Contents

Introduction

The purpose of this book is to offer teachers ideas and activities for integrating character education into their regular curriculum. The whole-group activities, games, art ideas, and more will help you teach character education in a fun way and help your students learn how to be caring and productive citizens. The activities can help build a sense of community in your classroom, and reinforce the importance of positive values for school and everyday life.

The following character traits are highlighted in this book: citizenship, compassion, fairness, honesty, integrity, perseverance, respect, responsibility, self-discipline, and trustworthiness. While each of the ten character traits is presented separately, it is important to understand that the ten traits together build a person of good character. As you discuss a character trait with your students, be sure to discuss how it relates to the other character traits and why it is important to exhibit all of the traits, and not just one or two. Each chapter includes the components listed below.

Definition of the Character Trait

Each chapter begins by defining a character trait. Along with the definition are specific ways for exhibiting the trait and the rewards that come with demonstrating the trait at home, school, and in one's community. The examples given are written in simplified terms so young students can gain a better understanding of how to apply this character trait to their own thoughts and actions. Read the introduction aloud to your students, and then take time to discuss the trait before moving on to the character-building activities. Refer back to the introduction as needed to reinforce the character trait definition and ways to exhibit the various positive behaviors.

Literature Suggestions

Enhance your character education activities by reading appropriate literature to the class. Literature selections for grades kindergarten through third grade are included for each character trait. Share all or several of these stories with your students and then discuss how characters in the stories exhibited the various character traits. If possible, place some of the recommended literature selections in your book center for students to look at and read during the study of each character trait.

Whole-Group Activities

Several options for whole-group activities are presented with each character trait. Games, songs, role playing, field trips, class projects, and more are included to add fun and excitement to your character education lessons.

2

Arts and Crafts Ideas

Detailed arts and crafts ideas are included for each character trait. Along with each idea is a materials list for easy reference, as well as complete directions and patterns (when necessary). Be sure to display your students' creations in your classroom throughout your study of each character trait.

Across-the-Curriculum Activities

Many of the activities included with each character trait can be easily integrated into other subject areas. Math, science, writing, language arts, and social studies can be reinforced through several of the character-building activities included with each chapter.

Bulletin Board Suggestions and Patterns

The bulletin board suggestions included with each character trait will compliment your lessons and provide a good visual resource for your classroom. Instructions are included for displaying each bulletin board, along with necessary patterns or directions for making your own bulletin board pieces. Display the bulletin board throughout the study of a character trait or longer for continuous visual reinforcement of each character trait.

Critical Thinking Exercises

To facilitate open-ended discussions about the various character traits, a critical thinking exercise is included in each chapter. By reading each of the situations given, and then allowing students to express their opinions and feelings to a variety of questions, your students will develop thinking, reasoning, and problem-solving skills that they can apply to everyday situations.

Citizenship

What Is Citizenship?

- Citizenship is having good manners and using kind words.
- Citizenship is obeying rules and respecting authority.
- Citizenship is accepting responsibility for your actions.
- Citizenship is what you do to make your home, school, neighborhood, and community better places.

How Can I Be A Good Citizen?

You can be a good citizen by using good manners. Saying "please" and "thank you," sharing with your friends, and taking turns are mannerly ways to act.

Showing care and concern through kind words is something a good citizen remembers to do. When you tell people that you like them, ask a friend to play with you, or tell your parents you appreciate them, you are showing that you care about the feelings of others.

A good citizen is someone who knows how to obey the rules at home, at school, and in the community. When you obey rules you are showing that you respect authority and those who make the rules. Many times rules are made so that everyone involved will be treated fairly and with respect. Rules are important because they keep people safe.

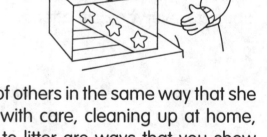

Voting on important issues is another way to show good citizenship. Issues can concern a small number of people (such as a classroom of students voting on a game to play during recess) or a great number of people (voting for leaders of a school, community, or even a country). Taking the time to vote is showing that you care about your community, which is an important part of being a good citizen.

A good citizen is someone who cares for the property of others in the same way that she would care for her own things. Handling a friend's toy with care, cleaning up at home, using school materials carefully, and remembering not to litter are ways that you show respect for someone else's property.

If you accept responsibility for your own actions, then you are showing good citizenship. Not following a rule, breaking someone's toy, or using unkind words are mistakes that we all make. By admitting mistakes and apologizing for them, you are showing that you want to improve your behavior. A good citizen is someone who is not afraid to admit that he is wrong and is always willing to ask for a second chance.

You belong to many different groups—your family, class, school, clubs, teams, and even your community. As a part of each of these groups, you should remember the steps to being a good citizen. Through your actions, you will demonstrate that you know what it takes to be a good citizen.

📖 Literature Selections

- **All in a Day** by Various Authors (Philomel Books, 1990)
- **Bully on the Bus** by Carl Bosh (Parenting Press, 1988)
- **Come Back Salmon: How a Group of Dedicated Kids Adopted Pigeon Creek and Brought it Back to Life** by Molly Cone (Sierra Club Juveniles, 1992)
- **Helping Out** by George Ancona (Clarion Books, 1985)
- **Spectacular Stone Soup** by Patricia Reilly Giff and Blanch Sims (Young Yearling, 1989)
- **The Car Washing Street** by Denise Lewis Patrick (William Morrow 1993)
- **The Gnats of Knotty Pine** by Bill Peet (Houghton Mifflin, 1984)
- **The Great Trash Bash** by Loreen Leedy (Holiday House, 1991)
- **The Messy Monster** by Michael Pellowski (Troll, 1989)
- **The Vote** by Linda Scher (Steck-Vaughn, 1996)

Good Citizen Signs

Materials:

- Good Citizenship pattern (page 14)
- chart paper and marker
- small paper plates
- craft sticks
- large box, basket, or other container
- crayons
- glue
- scissors

Reproduce one Good Citizenship pattern for each student. Let students give examples of how to be a good citizen (sharing, picking up trash, putting away toys, etc.) and examples of how not to be a good citizen (teasing friends, cheating, destroying property, etc.). Write the examples on a sheet of chart paper. Divide the class into groups of three. Give each group one bottle of glue, one pair of scissors, and some crayons, along with three copies of the Citizenship pattern, three craft sticks, and three paper plates. Ask the children to practice their good citizenship skills by sharing materials to color, cut out, and glue their patterns on their paper plates. As the students complete their signs, cut the chart (examples) into individual strips. Put the strips in a box or basket. Gather the children in a group circle. Have students bring their signs with them. Allow a student to pick a statement from the box and read it to the class. Ask the children to raise their signs if the statement is an example of good citizenship. Continue until all the statements have been read, or as time permits.

Applauding Good Citizenship

Materials:

- Hand pattern (page 14)
- construction paper strips, 3" wide, long enough to fit child's head
- crayons
- markers
- tape

Let each child cut out several handprint patterns and allow her to color or decorate and the handprints as desired. Then, have the children tape their handprints to their headbands. Allow the children to wear this Good Citizenship headband as they demonstrate good citizenship in the classroom.

Good Citizen Sing-Along

Materials:

- chart or chalkboard showing the words to the song (below)
- small rubber ball or beanbag

Song:

To the tune of "We Love You Dearly"

We are good citizens,
You know it's true.
We are good citizens,
In all we do,
We are good citizens,
Oh, yes it's true,
Good citizens in all we do.

Sing the song several times so the children are familiar with the words. Gather the class and have them sit in a circle. Pass the ball or beanbag around the circle as the entire group sings. When the song is finished, the student with the beanbag must give an example of something a good citizen would do (walk quietly in the hall, share toys, etc.), or tell how she has been a good citizen that day. The student then begins passing the ball again when the song starts. Continue to sing the song and give other students opportunities to respond. You may want to have someone write all the examples given and use them as a source for discussion or writing activities.

Good Citizens Quilt

Materials:

- yarn of different colors (red, black, brown, yellow), cut in various lengths
- wiggly eyes
- white fabric or tagboard squares, 10" x 10"
- hole punch
- paint pens or permanent markers
- glue
- scissors

Create a "quilt" that shows all members of your classroom community joined together. Have each student create a self portrait on a 10" x 10" square of fabric or tagboard. Let students add yarn pieces for hair and attach wiggly eyes to faces.

Punch holes around the edges of each square and "sew" the squares together with yarn. Each child can autograph his square with a paint pen or permanent marker. Then, display the completed quilt on a classroom or hall wall.

Community Guest

Invite someone from your school or community who demonstrates good citizenship skills to come and speak to your class. It could be a safety patrol member, school resource officer, the principal, or your hometown mayor. You might also want to invite an elected official who can discuss how he was elected by citizens in the community. Explain to your guest that your class has been studying good citizenship skills and that you would like for these to be addressed during the interview.

Before the visit, ask each student to come up with three questions she would like to ask the guest. (Younger children might practice with oral questions before their guest arrives.) Review questioning words such as "who," " what," "where," "when," and "why" with the students, along with rules for good listening. You might also want the students to record the speaker's answer to each question if time allows.

After the guest leaves, have the children list ways the speaker demonstrates that he is a good citizen. Have the children make thank-you cards to send to the guest. Point out that by sending thank-you's, they are practicing good citizenship, as well.

Vote for Good Citizenship

Materials:

- cardboard box
- large white paper, such as wrapping paper or craft paper
- small pieces of white paper or notebook paper
- scissors or craft knife
- crayons and markers
- pencils
- glue or tape

If possible, take students to a voting site during election time. Have someone show the class what is done with ballots or how a person's vote can be entered electronically.

Students may enjoy going through the motions of a mock election. Have the class make a ballot box by covering a cardboard box with white paper and cutting a slit in the lid. Then, let students decorate the box in patriotic or school colors. As a class, decide on issues about which the students would like to vote. If desired, have groups of students design election posters showing the various choices.

Provide students with small pieces of paper for marking their votes, then let them cast their vote in the ballot box. Count the votes and graph the results. Allow the class to vote on several different issues and then discuss the responsibility good citizens have to vote on issues.

Good Citizenship Banners

Materials:

- long strip of butcher paper
- student photographs or self-portraits
- laminator or clear self-adhesive paper
- write-on/wipe-off marker

During a class meeting at the beginning of the week, brainstorm with students to identify a citizenship goal that the class could adopt for the week. Goals such as walking quietly in the hall, completing homework assignments on time, or demonstrating good sportsmanship on the playground might be chosen. Have several choices available and then have the class vote on the one goal they would like to achieve.

Create a goal banner by decorating butcher paper with students' photographs or self-portraits. Laminate the banner or cover it with clear self-adhesive paper to create a write-on/wipe-off surface. When the class has chosen a goal for the week, have someone use an erasable marker to write the goal in the center of a banner. As you observe students demonstrating the citizenship goal during the week, add their names to the banner. Post the banner in the classroom to acknowledge your good citizens. At the beginning of the next week, wipe off the goal and names and begin the procedure again.

Citizenship Book

Materials:

- empty photo album
- markers, crayons, stickers, and other materials to decorate album cover

Bring a photo album to school and have the students work together to decorate the cover with the title "Good Citizens in Our Community." Invite the children to bring from home newspaper and magazine articles or pictures that show good citizenship. (You might want to send a letter to parents explaining what types of articles and pictures you are seeking. Examples could include a community litter pickup, a local election, a charity walk, etc.) Allow each child to share what he brings and then place the item in the photo album.

Good Citizen Chain

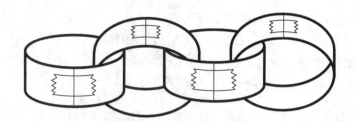

Materials:

- chalkboard and chalk or chart paper and marker
- strips of assorted colors of construction paper (12" x 1½")
- glue
- markers

Have your students talk about what makes someone a good friend and a good citizen. Help the class make a list of the different ways that they can demonstrate friendship and citizenship to their classmates.

Write the sentence starters from the list below on the chalkboard or chart paper, then ask students to use them to write sentences. After they have completed, reviewed, edited, and corrected their sentences, have each student copy one of his sentences onto a construction paper strip. Connect all the strips together by interlocking them and then gluing to make a "Good Citizen Chain." Display the chain in the classroom.

Sentence Starters:

- A good citizen is someone who...
- A good citizen will always...
- A good citizen never...
- You can trust a good citizen to...
- A good citizen will not...
- A good citizen tries to...
- A good citizen likes to...
- I am a good citizen when I...

Three-Word Poetry

Materials:

- pencils
- construction paper in a light color (9" x 12"), one per child

Have each child think of three "good citizenship words," such as "helpful," "concerned," "caring," etc. Give the child a piece of light-colored construction paper. Have him fold the paper into three horizontal sections. Then, direct the child to write one of his good citizenship words in each section and illustrate it. Have him fold the sections together (gate-style) and write, "A Good Citizen is...," on the outside cover of his poem.

10

GOOD CITIZENS HAVE HELPING HANDS

Reinforce the concept of community through this good citizenship bulletin board. Place the caption, "Good Citizens Have Helping Hands," in the center of your bulletin board. Make a copy of the hand pattern (page 14) for each student. On the patterns, let the students write examples of ways they show good citizenship. Let students share their examples as they are placed on the bulletin board around the caption.

         Citizenship

Name _____

 # Star Citizen Choices

Read each sentence. Circle YES if you think a good citizen would act this way. Circle NO if you do not think a good citizen would act this way. Then, on the back of your paper, rewrite each NO statement so that it becomes a YES statement.

1. Mike asks Ben if he can play on his team during P.E. Ben says, "I don't want you on my team. You're too slow." Is Ben being a good citizen?　　　YES　　　NO

2. Sally sees that Jane's glue bottle is empty and says, "Here Jane, you can use my glue." Is Sally being a good citizen?　　　YES　　　NO

3. Ricky is always pushing and shoving to get in the front of the line. Is Ricky being a good citizen?　　　YES　　　NO

4. Helen's school is voting on new colors for the basketball team uniforms. Helen says she doesn't have time to vote. When the colors are chosen, Helen complains that she doesn't like them. Is Helen being a good citizen?　　　YES　　　NO

5. Kevin borrowed Paul's airplane and broke it. He apologized and offered to pay Paul for it. Is Kevin being a good citizen?　　　YES　　　NO

6. When Kyle goes to the office to take a message for the teacher, he runs in the hall, even though he knows it is against the school rules. Is Kyle being a good citizen?　　　YES　　　NO

Note to Teacher: To make this worksheet appropriate for younger children, read the situations aloud and have students give a "thumbs up" or "thumbs down" to indicate whether the subject is being a good citizen or not.

Citizenship Critical Thinking

Read the following situation to the class. Ask the students the questions below for discussion.

Mrs. Rogers, a second grade teacher, asks Bruce and James to take some papers to the office for her. On the way to the office, Bruce runs in the hall. James follows the school rule and walks quietly. Then, Bruce goes into the boys' bathroom to wash his hands and he leaves the water running. James goes in to turn off the water, then reminds Bruce that they are not supposed to go anywhere but the office. All the way back from the office, Bruce runs in the hall. James reminds Bruce of the rules, but Bruce will not listen.

When the boys get back from the office, Mrs. Rogers says, "Did you both remember our good citizenship rules on the way to the office?" Bruce and James both answer, "Yes."

1. Do you think Bruce was acting like a good citizen in the hall? Why or why not?

2. Do you think James was acting like a good citizen in the hall? Why or why not?

3. How did James try to help Bruce while they were in the hall?

4. What do you think might have happened if James was not there to turn off the water?

5. Do you think you would act like Bruce or James if your teacher asked you to take papers to the office?

6. What should Bruce have done differently to show good citizenship?

Good Citizenship

Compassion

What Is Compassion?

- Compassion is caring about how others feel.
- Compassion is doing kind and thoughtful deeds for people in need.
- Compassion often means putting other people's needs before your own.

How Can I Show Compassion?

Compassion is something you show for others. When someone shows compassion, he shows that he cares about how others feel. A person can show compassion by being kind to others, helping those in need, and doing good deeds without expecting anything in return.

Sometimes we show compassion for people we know. Perhaps you have a friend who is feeling sad. You can show compassion by visiting your friend and listening to her talk about her sadness. A compassionate person understands when someone is feeling down and shows that he cares by being "a shoulder to cry on." By helping your friend feel better, you are showing compassion.

Sometimes we show compassion for strangers. There are many people in our world who need help obtaining food, clothing, shelter, or medical care. Whether these people in need are in your own community or on the other side of the world, you can show compassion by donating items that they need, helping build homes or shelter, or contributing money that will be used to buy necessary supplies.

Showing compassion is not always easy because often it means putting other people's needs before your own wants. For example, you may be asked to visit an elderly relative in the hospital when you had planned to play outside with your friends. By choosing to visit your relative, you are putting others' needs before your own—thereby showing compassion.

> **Your kind and caring actions can not only help others and make them feel better, but will make you feel proud of your good deeds. Compassion is a character trait that can benefit everyone.**

Literature Selections

- **Now One Foot, Now the Other** by Tomie de Paola (Putnam, 1988)
- **Special People (Who Cares)** by Rachel Letch (Child's Play International, 1995)
- **The Children's Book of Virtues** edited by William J. Bennett (Simon & Schuster, 1995)
- **The Giving Tree** by Shel Silverstein (Harpercrest, 1987)
- **The Rainbow Fish** by Mark Pfister (North-South Books, 1996)
- **The Selfish Giant** by Oscar Wilde (Simon & Schuster, 1984)

Compassion Cards

Materials:

- unlined 4" x 6" index cards
- pencils, crayons, and/or markers

Divide the class into pairs and give each pair several index cards, along with drawing tools. Have the pairs work together to draw or describe a scenario which might evoke a compassionate response (i.e., someone is homeless and without food). When the cards are complete, have each pair show their cards and discuss with the class the possible responses to the situations. This process should give the class a chance to generate many different types of compassionate responses.

My SISTER's favorite teddy-bear broke...

Adopt a Grandparent

Plan a class field trip to a nursing home center or care facility. Let students meet the residents. Before the visit, you may wish to have students think of questions to ask the residents. If the facility will allow, make arrangements for each child in the class to "adopt a grandparent" at the facility. Once a month throughout the school year, have students write letters to the "grandparents," make crafts for them, and visit their new friends.

Community Compassion

Materials:
- poster board
- markers or crayons
- several large cardboard boxes

Organize a school-wide clothing or food drive for a homeless shelter or other charitable organization in your community. Contact the organization to find out what donations it needs and set a date for delivery. Have students make posters promoting the drive, making sure to include lists of needed items, a "drop-off" location, and the deadline for donations. Display the posters in the classroom or throughout the school. At the drop-off site, make sure to have cardboard boxes or other containers for collecting the items. Let students sort the items if necessary, then have a parent volunteer to help deliver the items. Discuss with students what will happen to the donated goods and ask them how they feel about their compassionate good deeds.

Compassionate Story Starters

Use the following story starters and writing prompts in your writing center or during whole-group writing activities. Encourage students to express different ways that they can show compassion toward others. If desired, have students share their writing with the class or combine the pages into a class book. Keep the book at the writing center so that students may read each others' stories.

Story Starters:
- Once I helped a friend by...
- One way I have shown compassion is...
- When someone is sick, I can...
- Once someone showed compassion for me by...
- Once upon a time, there was a very compassionate boy/girl who...

People Who Care

Materials:
- local telephone books
- library resources

Invite children to use telephone books and library resources to locate names of charitable organizations, civic clubs, and other local or national groups that assist those in need. If possible, research together the history of a few of the organizations, such as the Red Cross or Salvation Army. Invite local representatives from the groups to come and speak with the students about the compassionate deeds of their organizations and volunteers.

Share Good Wishes

Materials:
- construction paper
- doilies, sequins, fabric, etc., to use in decorating greeting cards
- glue
- markers or crayons
- scissors

Ask students how we can show compassion to those who are sick or disabled. Emphasize acceptance and kindness. Have students use construction paper and craft materials to make get-well or cheer cards and pictures to send to sick patients in a local hospital.

Compassion

18

Compassion Acrostic

Materials:

- chart paper and marker
- dictionaries and/or thesauruses, optional

Have the class make an acrostic poem using the word "compassion." Write the word vertically on the left side of a sheet of chart paper, one letter per line. Then, have students dictate a sentence related to compassion using each of the letters. You may want to have them use dictionaries and thesauruses to find other words that relate to compassion.

Example:

Care for others!
Offer your help.
Make people happy.
Pay attention to feelings.
Always show compassion.
Send cards.
Sit with a sick friend.
Include others.
Other people matter.
Never be unkind.

Math Made Compassionate

Create word problems to coincide with the theme of compassion.

Examples:

- Simple operations: Mr. Perry's class was collecting coats to pass on to needy children. If three coats were collected on Monday and four were brought in on Tuesday, how many coats had been collected?

- Money: The coin drive for charity at Lakeshore Elementary raised 100 dimes, 576 pennies, 473 nickels, and 328 quarters. They also collected 3 fifty-cent pieces and 17 one-dollar bills. How much did they collect in all?
- Multiplication: Jenny and Michael collected canned goods for the homeless. If they collected 5 cans each day for 7 days, how many cans did they collect?

Compassion Goals

Materials:

- Compassion Goal Sheet (page 24)
- pencils

Reproduce the Goal Sheet so that each student has a copy. Ask students to fill in the dates for upcoming weeks. Let them illustrate the Goal Sheet borders and write a goal or activity for each week that would show compassion for others. Encourage students to review their goal sheets each week and concentrate on the goals they wrote.

At the end of four weeks, reward students with a special treat or prize.

"Cooking Up" Compassion

Materials:

- 9" paper plates, one per student
- construction paper circles cut to fit the paper plates
- ribbon, yarn, glitter, and/or other decorative craft materials
- glue
- pencils or markers
- scissors

Give each child a paper plate and a paper circle. Allow students to decorate the edges of the plates with ribbon, yarn, glitter, etc. On the paper circles, have children write what they think are the ingredients for compassion (i.e., one big hug, two parts giving, and a pinch of sympathy). Glue the paper circles on the paper plates. Display in the classroom on a bulletin board or by hanging from the ceiling.

Compassion Clown Bulletin Board

Display the Compassion Clown from page 25 as a reminder to students that they should practice compassion. Enlarge the clown pattern on page 25 and display it on a bulletin board. Reproduce and enlarge the balloon patterns from page 26 on brightly-colored construction paper so that each student will have one balloon. Have each student draw or write an example of an act of compassion on her balloon and attach it to a length of yarn or string. Attach each balloon to the bulletin board. Place some of the loose strings in the clown's hand and mount the balloons above the clown. Have students add balloons to the board as they observe or think of other compassionate acts.

Compassion Scramble

All the scrambled words below have to do with showing compassion. Unscramble them and write them in the blanks. Then, write sentences using each of the unscrambled words.

1. ringca _____

2. dink _____

3. flephul _____

4. efelgnis _____

5. ince _____

6. toehsr _____

7. refind _____

Note to Teacher: Cover the answers below before reproducing this page for students. For younger students, you may want to provide a word list from which to choose the answers. You might also write the scrambled words on a chalkboard or chart paper and work as a class to solve them. Answers: 1. caring; 2. kind; 3. helpful; 4. feelings; 5. nice; 6. others; 7. friend.

Critical Thinking

Share the following story with your class. Use the questions below for class discussion.

Robert and Caitlin were best friends in Ms. Crawford's third grade class. They talked on the telephone every night. One night, Robert could not reach Caitlin on the phone, even though he tried several times.

The next morning, Robert went to school only to find Caitlin was not there. Ms. Crawford told the class that the apartment building where Caitlin lived had burned last night.

Ms. Crawford said, "Caitlin and her mother are all right. Today, they are looking for a place to stay until the apartment is rebuilt. They lost almost everything they owned."

Robert and the rest of his classmates felt bad for Caitlin and her mother. Together, the class talked about ways they could help. Each child went home and talked to her parents about what had happened.

The next day, several of the students brought food to take to Caitlin. Some of them brought in clothes, towels, and coats. A few people even brought money to give to Caitlin's mother to buy things they needed. When the students looked at what they had, they realized they had enough food, clothing, and money to also give some items to the other people in the apartment building.

1. How do you think Robert felt when he could not reach Caitlin on the phone?

2. How do you think Caitlin felt after her home burned? How would you feel if this happened to you?

3. The class talked about ways they could help Caitlin and her mother. What do you think they said?

4. Why did the boys and girls decide to give to the other people in the building, even though they were strangers?

Compassion Goal Sheet

Name: _____

My Compassion Goals

Week 1: _____

_____

Week 2: _____

_____

Week 3: _____

_____

Week 4: _____

_____

Compassion Patterns

Compassion

Compassion Patterns

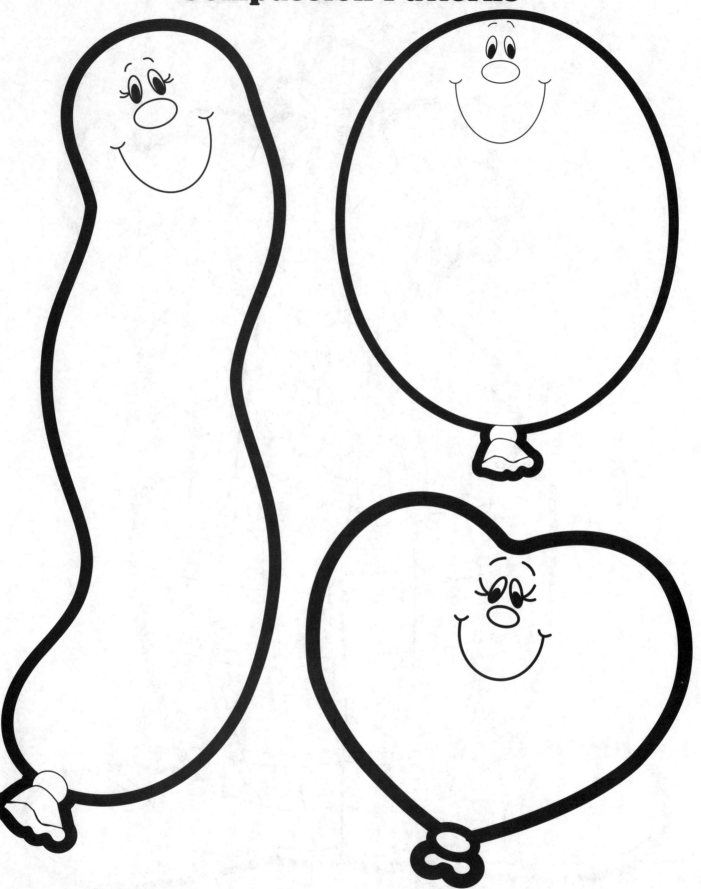

Fairness

What Is Fairness?

- Fairness means doing what is right to make sure others are not treated badly.
- Sometimes fairness means equal, but fairness does not always mean the same.

How Can I Show Fairness?

When you take turns, share, and listen to what others have to say, you are showing fairness to others. A fair person does not interrupt others when they are talking because fairness means waiting your turn. He does not keep a game or toy to himself when others are waiting to play because a fair person shares. He does not expect special treatment or favors because of who he is, but rather he works hard to be rewarded in a fair way.

People who are fair know that rules are made so everyone gets fair treatment. For example, a rule of raising your hand before talking in class gives everyone a chance to be recognized. It also assures that everyone can hear lessons since only one person talks at a time.

Sometimes fairness means "the same" or "equal." Perhaps there are two children and two cookies. It would be fair to give each child one cookie. It would not be fair to give one child both of the cookies and give the other child none. Consider a home with two brothers, however. One boy is thirteen years old and the other child is seven years old. The older brother has to mow the grass. The younger brother takes out the trash. This is also fair, even though it is not the same. Each child has a chore to do but the chores are not the same. The chores fit the age and ability of the children.

> **Fairness is playing by the rules, sharing, taking turns, and listening to what others say; it is giving every person the amount of time, energy, and respect that he deserves. The fair person knows that the best and most important reward he can receive is the feeling he gets inside when he does his best to treat others fairly.**

📖 Literature Suggestions

- **Chubbo's Pool** by Betsy Lewin (Clarion Books, 1996)
- **Connie Came to Play** by Jill Paton Walsh (Viking Children's Books, 1996)
- **The Doorbell Rang** by Pat Hutchins (Greenwillow Publishers, 1986)
- **It's Mine** by Leo Lionni (Dragonfly, 1996)
- **No Fair** by Caren Holtzman and Marilyn Burns (Cartwheel Books, 1997)
- **Playing the Game** by Kate Petty and Charlotte Firmin (Barrons Juveniles, 1991)
- **Rabbit and Hare Divide an Apple** by Harriet Ziefert (Viking Children's Books, 1998)

"Fairness Is the Way" Sing-Along

Materials:

- chalkboard and chalk, or chart paper and marker

Song:

Tune: "Here We Go 'Round the Mulberry Bush"

When we're at school, we share with others,
share with others, share with others.
When we're at school, we share with others.
Fairness is the way!

When we're at home, we do our chores...

When we're at play, we wait our turn...

Write the words to the song above on the chalkboard or chart paper. Sing the song until students are familiar with it. Allow the children to make up additional verses which reflect fairness. Ask older students to write sentences about how they are fair at home, school, and play. Have younger children draw pictures of the ways they are fair at home, school, and play.

Fair vs. The Same

Materials:

- chart paper and marker

Discuss as a class when "fair" means "the same." Discuss when it does not mean "the same." Draw a line down the middle of a sheet of chart paper. Write "Fair is the Same" at the top of one column. Write "Fair is Not the Same" at the top of the other column. Have children list things in the classroom which are the same for all children and the things that are not the same, but are fair, for all children in the classroom.

Examples:

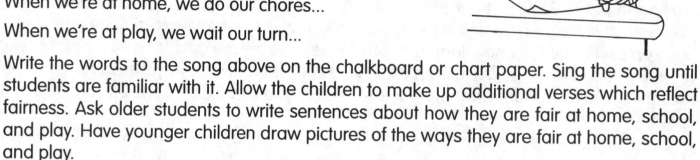

Fair is the Same

- All children must raise their hands before talking.
- All children must have their permission slips signed.
- All children must use polite language.

Fair is Not the Same

- All children can go to centers, but the centers are not the same.
- Everyone may check out a book from the library, but we each get a different book.
- Each child gets a chance to be a helper for a day, but each day's tasks may be different.

Fairness Everywhere

Materials:

- drawing paper
- crayons, markers

Before the activity, have a class discussion about fairness. Explain that fairness is a character trait they should show all of the time, everywhere they go. Then, divide the class into small groups. Assign each group an area of your school, such as the parking lot, the cafeteria, the media center, the classroom, the hallway, and the playground.

Once each child has been assigned to a group, have him draw a picture of himself being fair in that area. For example, a child in the media center group may draw himself turning in a library book on time so that others can read it, or waiting his turn in line at the computer. A child in the bus group could draw a picture of himself sitting quietly in his seat or offering to share a seat with another person. When the groups have finished their drawings, have each group share their pictures with the rest of the class.

Fair and Square

Materials:

- example of a square (manipulative or drawing)
- paper
- rulers
- pencils

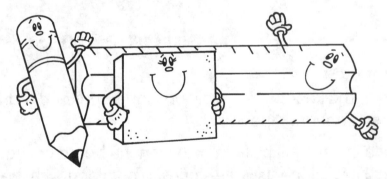

Ask your students what the phrase "fair and square" means. Hold up or draw on the chalkboard a picture of a square. Talk with your students about the attributes of a square and point out that all four sides of a square are equal.

Provide rulers, pencils, and paper to the students. Have the students draw several squares that are different sizes. (You might want to demonstrate use of the ruler for younger students.) If desired, tell your students what lengths to make the sides of their squares. For example, "Draw a square with two-inch sides." Reinforce the concept that all four sides must be equal. Afterward, talk about why squares might represent fairness and have each child write a sentence about something that is "fair and square." You may want to display the papers on a bulletin board titled "Fair and Square."

Fairness Desk Plates

Materials:
- Desk Plate patterns (page 37)
- strips of poster board, 3" x 16"
- old magazines, optional
- scissors
- glue

Let the children create desk plates about fairness using letters and symbols. Provide each child with a copy of the desk plate patterns. Have the children color and cut out the patterns, then glue them in order on their strips of poster board. Display the strips on the front of the children's desks.

Older students may enjoy cutting letters and symbols from old magazines and creating their own desk plates. Encourage them to be creative with abbreviations, sound-alike words, etc.

Stories about Fairness

Materials:
- chalkboard and chalk or chart paper and marker
- paper and pencils

Write the story titles from below on the board or chart paper. Allow each child to choose a title. Have students write stories to go along with the chosen titles and then share the stories with the class. If time allows, have the children draw pictures to illustrate the stories, then bind them into individual books or a class book.

Suggested Story Titles:
- How to Play Fair
- The Little Boy Who Cried, "It's Not Fair!"
- Two Apples, Three Children
- You're Not Old Enough
- Fairness Is the Way
- If Cinderella's Stepsisters Were Fair
- How I Would Make the World More Fair

Fairness Mobile

Materials:

- coat hanger for each child
- yarn or string, eight 6" lengths per child
- tagboard, eight 4" squares per child
- hole punch
- markers

Have children create mobiles using the word "fair." Give each student eight tagboard squares. On four of the squares, the students should write the word FAIR, one letter per square. Punch a hole at the top and bottom of each square.

Tie one length of the yarn or string to the bottom of the coat hanger. Loop the bottom of the string through the top of a letter square and then tie it in a knot. Continue until all of the letter cards are secured to the coat hanger in the correct order. Tie the other four pieces of yarn or string to the bottom holes of the cards.

Have students draw pictures showing fair situations on the four remaining squares. Punch a hole in the top of each card and tie the cards to the letter cards, one per letter, to complete the mobile.

Candy for All!

Materials:

- chart paper and marker
- one bag of candy-coated chocolate pieces or other small candies

Explain that "estimation" means making a guess about something. As a class, estimate how many pieces of candy are in the bag. Record each child's estimate on a chart. Count the candies. Divide them fairly and eat!

For an added challenge, have the class estimate and divide the candies by color.

The Fairness Game

Materials:

- chart paper and marker
- a variety of playground equipment and balls

Tell the children that they are to invent a new game. Give them the following guidelines for making the game fair:

- Use the same rules for everyone.
- Use the same equipment for everyone.
- Everyone gets a turn.
- The game is safe.

Play the game that the children invent. Review the game and fine-tune the rules if any unfairness was detected.

Example:

Put two bases 20 feet apart from each other for each of two teams. One child from each team must run from one base to the other, toss up a ball five times and catch it, and run back to the starting base. Run this as a relay until each child on both teams has had a turn. The first team to finish wins.

In this example, each team needs bases, each team needs a ball, the rules would be the same for everyone, and every child has a turn.

Doing Our Fair Share

Materials:

- chart paper with student names listed on it
- marker

Discuss with the students chores they do at home to help out. Ask if one person does all of the chores or if everyone pitches in. Ask what is the fair way to get chores done at home.

Display a piece of chart paper that lists the name of each student. Have the students brainstorm all the jobs and chores that must be done in the classroom during the day. As a job is named, write it beside the name of a student. Have the students continue to name jobs until every person in the class has an assignment. During the day, have the students perform their jobs. Praise students for doing their "fair share" in the classroom.

Our Fair Share

Materials:

- cookie mix and necessary ingredients, or refrigerated cookie dough
- cookie sheet
- oven
- bowl, spoon, and measuring cups, if using mix
- book, **The Doorbell Rang**, by Pat Hutchins (Greenwillow, 1986), optional

Make a batch of cookies for the class (double recipe for larger classes). If possible, allow students to make the cookies while you reinforce measurement and cooking concepts. When the cookies are cooled, have the class count how many are in the batch. Ask the class to decide how to fairly divide the cookies. Divide and eat. (If desired, challenge the students to divide the cookies into different amounts. Younger students can give each child one cookie and then brainstorm what to do with the remaining cookies.) As a follow-up, you may want to read **The Doorbell Rang**, by Pat Hutchins (Greenwillow, 1986), to the class.

Fairness Necklace

Materials:

- Fairness Necklace pattern (page 37)
- two colors of yarn, cut to necklace length and tied, one per child (half the class should have one color and the other half of the class should have the other color)
- markers or crayons
- tape
- scissors

As the children enter the classroom one morning, give each child one yarn necklace. During the morning, let the group with one color necklace be first in line, do special activities, be helpers, etc. (Do not call attention to their special privileges.)

At the end of the morning, call the class together to discuss how each group feels about how they are being treated. Have the students name some things that were unfair during the morning and why. Ask the children in the "special" group if they felt bad for their friends who were being treated unfairly.

To make each group "equal," let each child add a Fairness Pendant to her necklace. Give each child a pattern. Let students color the patterns, cut them out, and tape them to their necklaces. Have the students wear the pendant necklaces for the rest of the day as reminders that "fairness is the way to play."

Place light-colored background paper (preferably yellow) on the bulletin board. Use black paper strips or a black marker to create a "ruler" on the board. If possible, make the ruler to scale. (You might want to have your students help you design the ruler for an integrated lesson on measurement and proportion.)

Have students draw scenes that show fairness, or cut scenes depicting fairness from old magazines. Let children place the pictures on and around the ruler.

Suggested Captions:
- Fairness Rules!
- Rules to Fairness
- Measuring Fairness
- We're Working to be "Fair and Square"

Riddle Worksheet

To answer the riddle, color the squares in the puzzle, following the color code below.
What did the little boy show to his friends when they asked to play with his toy?

Color each L red.
Color each T blue.
Color each G green.
Color each V orange.

Color each B black
Color each O yellow.
Color each X purple.
Color each K brown.

F	L	T	B	O	X	L	G
T	A	K	X	K	O	V	B
G	X	I	L	T	G	X	T
V	L	V	R	K	O	V	L
B	O	K	O	N	B	T	O
V	K	T	B	G	E	X	G
T	B	O	V	T	V	S	K
O	X	G	L	V	B	O	S

Can you see the answer? Draw a picture to go along with the riddle.

Critical Thinking

Read the following story to the class. Have the children respond to the questions below for class discussion.

One day, Jan and Philip's grandmother took the twins out for an ice cream treat. Grandmother told the children that they could have two scoops of ice cream each. Jan complained that the last time she came to the ice cream store she was allowed three scoops. She said that it wasn't fair for Grandmother to only let her have two scoops. As Grandmother was explaining that two scoops were plenty, Jan interrupted her and would not let her finish. Jan finally ordered her two scoops.

When the ice cream arrived, Jan said that Philip's scoops were bigger than hers when really they were about the same size. She said it wasn't fair that Philip's scoops were bigger than hers. Grandmother told Jan that she was the one who was being unfair.

1. Why do you think Grandmother wanted to take Jan and Philip for an ice cream treat?

2. Was it unfair that Jan was only able to get two scoops of ice cream? Why or why not?

3. How do you think Grandmother felt about Jan's behavior?

4. What did Grandmother mean when she told Jan that she was the one who was being unfair?

5. What can Philip and his grandmother do to help Jan learn about fairness?

6. How could this story end to show Jan finally being fair?

Fairness Patterns

Desk Plate Patterns

Fairness Necklace Pattern

Fairness

Honesty

What Is Honesty?

- An honest person is someone who tells the truth.
- An honest person does not cheat, steal, or lie.

How Can I Be an Honest Person?

Whether at home, school, or the playground, an honest person always does his best to tell the truth. An honest person knows that lying to others is wrong and can hurt their feelings. Truthful words and truthful actions are important parts of honesty.

An honest person does not steal or cheat. He knows that stealing is wrong. He would never take a toy, candy, money, or anything that does not belong to him. Rules and laws about stealing are made to keep everyone's property safe. An honest person would not want to break these rules or laws. Cheating is also something that an honest person would not do. Copying someone else's paper is not right. Doing your own work and trying to do your best shows honesty.

An honest person keeps his promises. When an honest person says that he will do a chore or job for someone, he always does it to the best of his ability. An honest person makes sure that he completes the job the way that he was asked to.

> **Many people say, "Honesty is the best policy." This statement means that it is very important to always tell the truth and never steal or cheat. If you are an honest person, your character will shine through and you will feel good about your actions. Make honesty your policy!**

📖 Literature Selections

- **A Big Fat Enormous Lie** by Marjorie Weinman Sharmat (EP Dutton, 1993)
- **Anteater on the Stairs** by Peter Coltrill (Kingfisher Books, 1994)
- **Believing Sophie** by H. J. Hutchens (Albert Whitman and Co., 1995)
- **Honest Tulio** by John Himmelman (Bridgewater Books, 1997)
- **Lleonard, The Llama that Lied** by Susan Cameron (Paulist Press, 1997)
- **Nina, Nina, Star Ballerina** by Jane O'Conner (Grosset & Dunlap, 1997)
- **Rufus's Big Day** by Jane Luck WIlson (Ozark Publishing, 1996)
- **The Boy Who Cried Wolf** by Tony Ross (Penguin, 1992)

Honesty Sing-Along

Practice singing the song to the right until the class is familiar with it. Have the children form a large circle. Pick two children to form a bridge in the middle of the circle by holding hands and raising their arms. Pick five or six children to go under the bridge as the rest of the class sings the song. On the last line, have the bridge children "capture" a student by bringing down their arms and encircling her. The student who is captured must give an example of a time when she or someone else was honest. Have someone record each answer on the chalkboard or chart.

Song:

To the tune of "London Bridge"

Honest people tell the truth, tell the truth, tell the truth.

Honest people tell the truth.
I am honest!

Honest people never cheat...

Honest people never steal...

Totem Poles of Honesty

Materials:

- oatmeal canisters or large cans, one per student
- construction paper
- feathers, tissue paper, buttons, and yarn (optional)
- glue
- markers
- tape
- scissors

Explain that in Native American cultures, honesty is stressed in daily living. Many believe that honesty helps create harmony in the tribe. A Native American totem pole contains carvings representing a community or tribe. Create class totem poles which depict the classroom community's pride in being honest.

Give each child an oatmeal canister or can and construction paper. Have him cover his container with the construction paper. Then, let him decorate the paper by adding facial features using markers, craft materials, or additional construction paper. Have each child trace both of his hands on construction paper, cut them out, and attach them to the sides of the can. Have the child write a poem or story about how it makes him feel to be honest. Attach this to the back of the can. Tape four or five cans, one on top of another, to finish each totem pole. Display in the classroom.

Ask the children to look at "Totem Poles of Honesty" each day as they enter the classroom as a reminder to always be honest.

Signs of Honesty

Materials:

- Honest/Dishonest Card patterns (page 47)
- wooden craft sticks
- 3" x 5" pieces of construction paper, one per student
- crayons or colored markers
- glue
- scissors

Discuss the words "honest" and "dishonest" with the class. Give each child one "Honest" card pattern and one "Dishonest" card pattern, along with a piece of construction paper. Have each child color, cut out, and glue the cards on opposite sides of the construction paper, then glue a craft stick to the paper as a handle.

Read the following situations and instruct the children to hold up the correct side of their signs to indicate the type of behavior described.

- Jenny goes to the store to buy some milk for her mother. On the way out of the store she realizes that the cashier made a mistake and gave her too much change. She is excited because she now has money to go by the ice cream shop on the way home. Is Jenny being honest?

- Steven forgot to study for his math test. Jan, an excellent student, is sitting in the desk beside Steven, and Steven can see Jan's test paper easily. Steven knows that he needs to make a good grade on the test, but he does not copy Jan's paper because he believes in doing his own work. Is Steven being honest?

- Sammy likes to go to Kevin's house and play with Kevin's toy cars. Kevin has about 30 cars in his collection. One day while Sammy is visiting Kevin he slips a red car in his pocket while Kevin is not looking. He doesn't think that Kevin will miss it because he has so many. Is Sammy being honest?

- Kelly, Julie, and Sarah go shopping. Their last stop is the drug store. Sarah hears Kelly and Julie giggling at the nail polish counter. When she walks up, she sees that they are putting bottles of nail polish in their pockets. Kelly tells Sarah that she should take one too. Sarah says, "No, that is stealing and it is not the right thing to do." Is Sarah being honest?

Take time for discussion after the children have indicated their view of each situation. Ask the children how the dishonest situations could be turned into honest ones.

As an alternative, pairs or groups of children could act out each situation and their classmates could indicate their opinions with their puppets. You might also have children write additional situations to discuss.

The Boy Who Cried Wolf

Materials:

- book, **The Boy Who Cried Wolf** by Tony Ross (Penguin, 1992)

Share with students the story of **The Boy Who Cried Wolf**. Discuss with the class the ways in which the boy showed dishonesty. Children might want to try reenacting the story or creating stick puppets of the characters. After telling or reenacting the story, ask the students the following questions.

- Why did the boy call for help the first time?
- How did the villagers feel when they got to the top of the hill and the boy was laughing?
- Why did the villagers ignore the boy's last call for help?
- Do you think the boy will play tricks on others again? Why or why not?
- What would have happened if the boy had never played a trick on the villagers?

Honesty Web

Materials:

- chalkboard and chalk or chart paper and marker
- book or books from Literature Selections list (page 38)

To get your students to focus on honesty as a character trait, have them complete an honesty web using a story from the Literature Selections list.

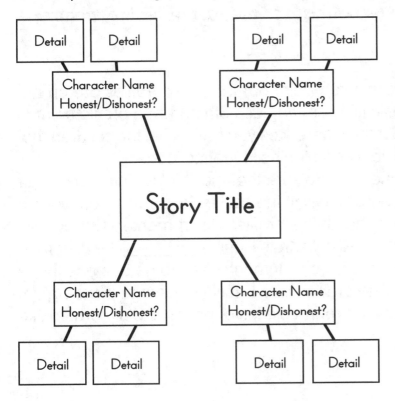

On the chalkboard or chart paper, draw a web like the one illustrated at left. Share a story with the class, then work together to fill in the web. The title of the story should be written in the center of the web. In the boxes that surround the title, write the names of the story characters, and write "honest" or "dishonest" to describe each character. In the boxes radiating from the character names, write short phrases to indicate what each character did to show that he was honest or dishonest.

After doing this activity as a class, you may want to give individual children copies of an honesty web to fill out while they are reading a story independently.

Profile Silhouettes

Materials:

- 12" x 18" construction paper in two contrasting colors
- light source
- glue
- tape
- marker
- scissors

George Washington and Abraham Lincoln are remembered for living honest lives. Share with the class the legends of how George Washington and Abe Lincoln showed honesty:

George Washington was said to have always told the truth. When he was a young boy he got a hatchet for a gift. He went outside and used it to cut down one of his father's cherry trees. His father was very angry when he found out that someone had cut down his tree. When he asked George about it, George replied, "Father, I cannot tell a lie. I chopped down the tree."

Once, when Abraham Lincoln was a child, he went to the store for his mother. On the way home he discovered that he had received too much change. Instead of keeping the money for himself, he walked all the way back to the store and returned the change. Even though it was a long way back to the store, Abe did not want to keep something that was not his. For the rest of his life, people knew him as "Honest Abe."

As you discuss these famous Americans, you can point out that their profiles are on our coins. Discuss with your class what a profile is. Examine each other from a profile point of view and a full face point of view. Talk about the differences you notice. Tell the children that they are special and that you want to acknowledge their silhouettes too.

Tape a piece of construction paper to the wall. Be sure that the child is sitting in a chair close to the wall so that the shadow of her profile will fit the paper. Set up your light source to cast a shadow on the paper and trace the child's profile with a marker. Cut out the silhouette and glue it onto contrasting paper. Title the portrait "Honest _____(child's name)"

Older children can write character biographies about themselves to go along with the silhouettes or write sentences telling how they are like Abe Lincoln or George Washington.

Alternatively, silhouettes can be mounted on round pieces of paper and decorated like coins.

Honesty Pledge

Materials:

- construction paper
- tissue paper
- glitter
- ribbon
- yarn
- markers
- glue
- masking tape
- scissors

Explain to students that a pledge is a promise to do something. Ask if they are familiar with the Pledge of Allegiance or other pledges such as the Girl Scout or Boy Scout pledge. An "honesty pledge" is a promise to yourself and others that you will be honest in all you do. This project will help students make the honesty pledge and remind them that honesty is always the best policy.

For each pledge, cut construction paper in a banner shape as illustrated above. Cut an 18" length of yarn for each banner. Attach the yarn to the banner by taping the ends to the back of the paper. Instruct the child to mark off a two-inch border around the outside of the banner. Have the child make a decorative border with markers, yarn, tissue paper, construction paper, etc. Title the banner "_____'s Honesty Pledge." Inside the border, the student should write four things he can do to show that he is honest. Display the banners in the classroom or send them home to share with parents.

Class Honesty Book

Materials:

- chalkboard and chalk or chart paper and marker
- two sheets of construction paper
- writing paper
- pencils
- stapler, or hole punch and yarn
- markers or crayons
- laminator or clear, self-adhesive paper

On the chalkboard or chart paper, write several story starters like those below. Give each student paper and a pencil, then ask her to choose a story starter and write a story to go with it. Have students work together to design a front cover for a class book, using construction paper and markers or crayons. Laminate the front cover and a second sheet of construction paper which will be the back cover, or cover both pieces with clear, self-adhesive paper. Bind the students' stories between the covers using a stapler, a hole punch and yarn, or a binding machine. Place the book in your class library for everyone to enjoy.

Story Starters:
- Yesterday I found $100...
- During the test, my friend asked for the answers...
- Telling the truth means...
- My little brother told me a lie...
- Honesty is important because...

"Badge of Honesty" Bulletin Board

Officer Cremins and the Honesty Patrol

Floyd · Rebecca · Travis · Anne · Margaret · Shelly · Alice · Pablo · Jason · Alvin · Michael · Denise · T.J. · Matt · Dion · Caroline

This bulletin board will show your appreciation of your students' honesty. Cover your bulletin board with light paper. Enlarge and color the Police Officer pattern (page 47). Display it on the board. Using the Badge patterns on page 47 (enlarge if desired), create gold badges from metallic paper or yellow construction paper. Write each student's name on a badge, then mount the badges on the bulletin board.

When you observe a student in a situation that indicates her honesty, reward her by placing a gold foil star on her badge (or drawing a star with a marker). The children will be excited to see themselves as members of the "Badge of Honesty Team"!

Suggested Captions:
- Join Our Honesty Patrol!
- We Show Our Honesty!
- We Are Proud of Our Honesty!
- The Honesty Patrol
- A Badge for Honesty
- Calling the Honesty Patrol!

Name _____

Honesty Scenarios

Look at each picture below. Circle "yes" if you think the picture shows something an honest person would do. Circle "no" if you think the picture shows something an honest person would not do.

YES   NO

YES   NO

YES   NO

YES   NO

Pick one of the illustrations that shows someone being dishonest. Write a sentence or draw a picture to show how this person should act in an honest way.

45

Honesty

Critical Thinking Activity

Share the following story with your class. Use the questions below for discussion.

Mary lives near a park. Every day at 2:00 the ice cream truck stops by a bench in the park. On Monday Mary's mother gave her $1.00 to buy an ice cream cone. The man in the ice cream truck gave her change back and she sat down on the bench to eat her ice cream. When Mary finished she counted her change and realized that the man had given her too much money back. The ice cream truck had already left.

1. What should Mary do to show that she is honest? Why?

2. Have you ever been in a similar situation? How did you feel? What did you do?

3. Does it really matter to the man on the ice cream truck if he doesn't get the change back? Why or why not?

4. Does the amount of money involved make a difference in how you should react to a situation like this? Why or why not?

5. What if the ice cream man had given Mary too little change? Should she handle it differently?

Honesty Patterns

Honest

Dishonest

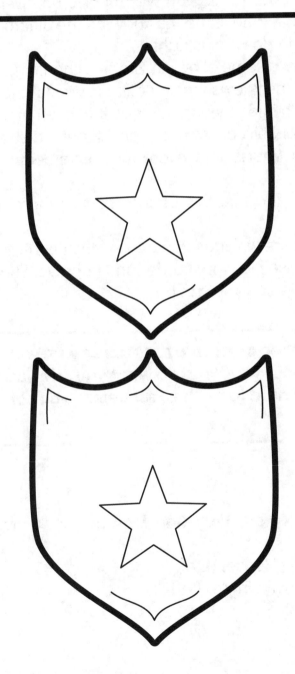

Honesty

Integrity

What Is Integrity?

- Integrity means being strong enough to do what you know is right.
- Integrity means knowing the difference between right and wrong and choosing to do the right thing, even when it is difficult.

How Can I Show Integrity?

Integrity is a big word that means doing what you know is the right thing to do. It is standing up for what you believe in. Integrity is having standards that you will not give up, even in difficult times. It means being honest and telling the truth. It means knowing the difference between right and wrong, and always choosing to do what is right.

An example of integrity would be if a person sees some of his classmates cheating on a test. Although he might be tempted to cheat also, he knows that cheating is wrong and he decides to do his own work instead. A person with integrity understands that even though other people are doing the wrong thing, he should still do what is right. A person shows integrity by having confidence in his decision to do what is right, even when other people try to make him do wrong.

A person with integrity admits his mistakes and tries his best to correct them. He does not blame others for his actions.

Having integrity also means trying and learning new things. A person with integrity tries to do just a little better each time, challenging himself to work harder and improve. Showing integrity means working hard to be the best person you can be.

When you do what you know is right, even when others may not agree with you, you are showing integrity. When you keep your word and do what you say, you are showing integrity. Integrity means trying hard to be the best person you can be.

📖 Literature Selections

- **Alexander and the Terrible, Horrible, No Good, Very Bad Day** by Judith Viorst (Athaneum, 1972)
- **Duck, Duck, Goose?** by Katya Arnold (Holiday House, 1997)
- **Ruby the Copycat** by Peggy Rathman (Scholastic Trade, 1991)
- **The Magic Fan** by Keith Baker (Voyager, 1997)

Yes/No Game

Materials:
- two large pieces of paper
- marker
- masking tape

Create two signs by writing the word "yes" on one large piece of paper and the word "no" on another. Have the children stand in an open space in the classroom. Place a piece of masking tape on the floor to divide the area into two sections. Place a sign in each section. Give your students examples of situations in which someone's integrity is tested and have them decide what they would do in each situation. Encourage the children to be honest and allow them to explain their answers.

Examples:
- Matt and his friends went to the movies. His friends snuck in the side door without paying. Should Matt sneak in, too?
- Your friends have been stealing gum from the store. They want you to steal some gum, too. Do you steal the gum?

Other situations might include cheating on a test, teasing, breaking a neighbor's window, littering, and skipping school. Have the children listen to the situation and stand on either the "yes" or "no" side of the tape to indicate their answers, then let them explain their responses.

Fishing for Integrity

Materials:
- Fish pattern (page 56)
- fish bowl or other container
- pencils or markers
- crayons

Reproduce the fish pattern so that each child has one. Have students write their names on the fish, then color them. Place the fish in a fish bowl or other container. Gather the class in a circle and let students take turns pulling fish from the bowl. As a child pulls a fish out, he should read the name and then tell one way that student displays integrity (i.e., follows the rules, does not run in the hall, follows directions, does not cheat, does not lie, is kind to others).

Afterward, you may want to display the fish on a bulletin board or door with a caption such as "Fishing for Integrity."

Integrity Pennants

Materials:

- chalkboard and chalk or chart paper and marker
- 9" x 12" white construction paper, cut diagonally in half
- straw, dowel, or unsharpened pencil for each student
- crayons or colored markers
- tape or glue
- scissors

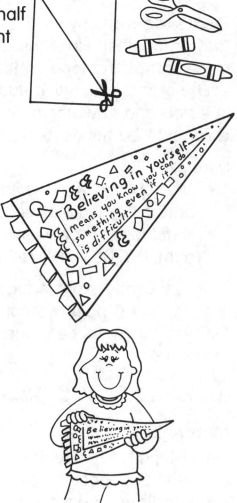

Have the children help you think of sentences that describe integrity (see suggestions below). Write the sentences on the chalkboard. Let each child choose a sentence and write it on a piece of white paper which has been cut into a triangle shape to resemble a pennant. Then, at the bottom of the pennant, have the child write about what his chosen sentence means. For example, if the child chose the sentence, "Believe in yourself," he could write, "Believing in yourself means that you know you can do something, even if it is difficult." Have the child decorate the pennant, then tape or glue it to a straw, dowel, or pencil and proudly wave his "integrity banner"!

Suggested phrases:

- Always do your best.
- Be the best person you can be.
- Believe in yourself.
- Do the right thing.

Challenge Yourself

Materials:

- sentence strips (one for each child)
- pencils or markers
- tape

Talk with the children about challenging themselves to always do what is right. Explain that sometimes it may be difficult to do what is right, but a person with integrity meets the challenge of doing the right thing anyway. Give each child a sentence strip. Have the child write a sentence naming something that is the "right thing to do." For example, "It is right to always do your own work," or, "Being kind to others is the right thing to do." Have the students attach their sentence strips to their desks, and then challenge them to do the things they wrote. Each time you see a student meeting her challenge, draw a "smiley" face or attach a sticker on her sentence strip. When students have received a predetermined number of smiles, reward them with small treats.

Words of Integrity

Materials:

- 13 sheets of construction paper
- marker

Write each letter from the words "show integrity" on a separate sheet of construction paper, filling the whole sheet with the letter. Place the letters in the chalkboard tray or on the floor. Have students take turns forming new words with the letters. Then have the students use each word in a sentence. Example: I **grin** when I show integrity.

Act It Out

Materials:

- 35 cents (real or toy money)

Read the story below to the class. Pair up the students and give them plastic or real money as a prop. Let each pair take a turn acting out how they would finish the story. Have the class decide which characters show integrity.

Sandy and John are twins who sit next to each other in class. Both Sandy and John like to buy ice cream at lunch, but their parents only give them enough money to get the treat once a week. One morning, while sharpening her pencil, Sandy found 35 cents on the floor. That was just enough for a chocolate ice cream cup, her favorite. John knew she had already bought ice cream this week.

Finish the story by acting out how you would handle this situation, showing the trait of integrity.

What Is Integrity?

Materials:

- 9" x 12" construction paper
- pencils, crayons, or markers

Talk with the children about what integrity means. Explain that integrity means many things, including being honest, taking responsibility, and doing what is right. Give each child a piece of 9" x 12" construction paper. Have him fold the paper once vertically and then again horizontally to create a "book." Have the child write the word "Integrity" on the front of the book. On the inside pages he should write, "Be honest." and "Be responsible.", and on the back page, "Do what is right." For each page have the child illustrate and dictate a sentence about the heading. Let the children write their names on their books and then share the books during reading or sharing time.

Integrity Song

Sing to the tune of "Three Blind Mice."

Integrity, integrity.
Do what is right.
Do what is right.
Be honest and truthful. Know right from wrong.
Be the best you can be as it says in this song.
You know what is right, be the best you can be.
Integrity, integrity.

What Is Right? and What Is Wrong?

Materials:

- 9" x 12" construction paper
- crayons or markers

Talk with the children about how a person with integrity acts. Give each child a 9" x 12" piece of construction paper. Have him fold the paper in half. In the first section, have him illustrate a scene showing a person doing something that does not show integrity. Then, beside this picture, have him draw another illustration showing a person doing something that shows integrity. An example for the first picture could be, "A person who hits others does not show integrity." An example for the second picture could be, "A person who always treats others kindly shows integrity."

"Bee" the Best Bulletin Board

"Bee" the Best Person You Can Be!

Give each child a piece of white construction paper, approximately 5" x 7". Have him draw a picture of himself and color it using crayons or markers. Give each child a 6" x 8" piece of construction paper and a copy of the bee pattern from page 56. Instruct him to place his self-portrait in the middle of the construction paper and trace around the edges. Have him cut out the traced square in the middle of the paper to create a picture frame. Have him then tape his picture inside the frame. Let him color and cut out a bee pattern and glue it to the corner of the frame. Display all the completed pictures on a bulletin board display titled "'Bee' the Best You Can Be!" If desired, enlarge and decorate several bee patterns as well as the hive pattern on page 57 to complement the display.

Name _____

Integrity Match

Draw a line to the phrase which will complete each sentence to show integrity.

1. When I know something is wrong,

2. When I say I will do something,

3. When someone asks me something,

4. When I know something will hurt another person's feelings,

6. When I see someone stealing,

7. When I accidentally break something,

8. When someone tells me to do something that is wrong,

5. When I see someone cheating on a test,

I do it anyway.
I do not do it.

I keep my word.
I forget about it.

I tell the truth.
I tell a lie.

I do not say it.
I say it anyway.

I steal also.
I tell a person who can help.

I blame someone else.
I take responsibility and try to fix it.

I tell them, "No."
I say, "OK."

I do my own work.
I cheat, too.

Note to Teacher: To make this worksheet appropriate for younger children, read the situations aloud and have students give oral responses.

Critical Thinking Activity

Share the following story with your class, then use the questions below as follow-up.

Jim and his friends Anthony and Dave always went to the corner store after school to buy candy. One afternoon while at the store, Jim saw his friend Anthony put some candy in his pocket without paying for it.

Anthony whispered to Jim and Dave, "Take some candy. We won't get caught."

Dave grabbed some candy and quickly put it in his pocket, but Jim said, "We have to pay for the candy. Stealing is wrong. If you don't put it back or pay for it, I am going to tell the cashier what you did."

Anthony and Dave put the candy back. When they left the store, the boys told Jim they were angry with him. Although Jim did not want his friends to be angry with him, he could not let them steal. He knew he had done the right thing.

1. What did Jim do that showed he had integrity?

2. Why did Jim feel like he had to stop his friends from stealing the candy?

3. If his friends took the candy anyway, what could Jim have done?

4. If Jim had walked away and let the boys steal the candy, would he have shown integrity? Why or why not?

5. If the boys stole the candy and did not get caught, would it have been the right thing to do? Why or why not?

Integrity Patterns

Integrity Patterns

Integrity

Perseverance

What Is Perseverance?

- Perseverance helps someone stick with an activity until it is finished.
- Perseverance is not giving up.
- Perseverance is staying with something even when others might quit or give up.

What are Some Examples of Perseverance?

An example of perseverance would be when you are running a long race. In the course of the race, you might fall, you might see others stop or leave the race, or your legs might burn and your heart begin to pound. You may feel that you cannot go another step. Something inside you says, "Keep going." You persevere to the finish line. You may not win the race, but you keep going until you finish.

Perseverance could also be continuing to work on a problem until you get the correct answer. You may have a math worksheet that is very hard for you. You may have to ask for help with the problems or you may have to put the paper aside for a while and then come back to it at a later time. You keep working at the problems until they are correct. You have persevered in your school work.

When you are just learning to ride a bicycle without training wheels, you persevere until riding becomes easy. At first, it may be very difficult. You may fall off the bike several times, and may even get scrapes and bruises, but you keep trying, over and over, until you can ride the bicycle with ease.

Perseverance is the character trait that helps you stick with an activity even if it is difficult or long. It is a trait that requires a great effort but provides a rewarding feeling.

📖 Literature Selections

- **Angus and the Cat** by Marjorie Flack (Farrar, Straus & Giroux; 1997)
- **Brave Irene** by William Steig (Farrar, Straus & Giroux; 1986)
- **Hard to Be Six** by Arnold Adof (Lothrop, Lee & Shepard, 1991)
- **Ox-Cart Man** by Donald Hall (Viking Children's, 1979)
- **The Hare and the Tortoise** by Carol Jones (Houghton-Mifflin, 1996)
- **The Little Engine that Could** by Watty Piper (Platt and Munk, 1991)
- **The Very Quiet Cricket** by Eric Carle (Putnam Publishing Group, 1997)

Stick with It

Ask students how the phrase "Stick with it" reminds them of perseverance. Then, invite the students to play a game called Stick with It. Begin the game like tag, with one person designated as "It." Stick with It begins as "It" chases the other children. When the first child is tagged, she must link arms with "It." The next tagged child links arms with the first child, and so on, to make a chain. The children must "stick together" as they chase the remaining students. The last child tagged becomes "It" for the next game.

"Working Hard" Sing Along

Materials:
- chart paper and marker

Song:
To the tune of "Mary Had a Little Lamb"

When you're working, stick with it, stick with it, stick with it.
Keep on going, do your best. Don't give up!

When you're playing...

When you're running...

When you're learning...

Make a chart with the words from the song above. Sing the song until children are familiar with it. Allow children to come up with additional verses, naming things which require perseverance.

Perseverance Puzzle

Materials:
- sentence strips
- marker
- scissors

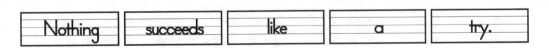

| Nothing | succeeds | like | a | try. |

Make sentence strips with sentences about perseverance, such as: "If at first you don't succeed, try, try again;" "Nothing succeeds like a try;" "Hard work brings good results;" etc. Cut the words of each sentence apart to make a puzzle, and allow the class to put the words in order. Have students read the sentences and tell you what they mean.

Pioneer Spirit

Materials:

- blue construction paper
- blue tissue paper
- blue crayons and markers
- blue yarn, buttons, pipe cleaners, and/or other blue craft materials
- glue
- scissors

Discuss with the children how the pioneers of long ago persevered through hard times and bad conditions to settle in new lands. People from many countries came to the United States to find freedom and a better life. Times were often very hard but, through perseverance, the pioneers stayed dedicated to their dreams.

Ask the children if they can name a symbol for America. Tell them that the American flag is one symbol that not only represents the land, but also the people of America. The colors of the flag are sometimes said to have been chosen to represent the traits of the American people. Red represents courage, white represents innocence, and blue represents perseverance. Ask the children why they think perseverance was chosen as a trait to be represented on the flag. Then, provide the following to the students: blue construction paper, blue tissue paper, blue crayons, blue markers, and other blue materials. Have the students use glue and scissors to construct their own blue symbols for perseverance.

We All Persevere

Materials:

- basket or box
- paper and pencils

Write each child's name on a long strip of paper and place it in a basket or box. Let each child draw a name and then write one sentence on the strip about how the person whose name he drew shows perseverance. Place all of the strips back in the basket and draw out one sentence at a time to read aloud. Let the class guess who is the subject of the sentence.

Examples:
- Marie: Works hard on math problems.
- Ryan: Cleans the home center very well.
- Lynn: Takes her time on her handwriting.

Hard-Working Animals

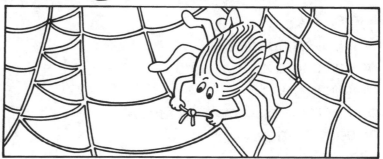

Materials:

- a variety of books, pictures, and other resources about animals
- stamp pad with washable ink
- paper
- colored markers

Allow your students to learn about how some animals show perseverance through instinctive (unlearned) habits. Gather books, pictures, and other resources on animals. Here are some suggested animals and topics to study:

- Baby chicks: It may take hours for a baby chick to break through its shell. Discuss how this small creature—even during its first day—works hard to break through.
- Beavers: A beaver uses its teeth to cut down trees and build a dam or lodge. Through hard work, the beaver uses mud, rocks, limbs, and logs to build the structure.
- Birds: Some birds build elaborate structures in trees, holes in the ground, buildings, or bushes. These structures—nests—are the result of hard work and time spent hunting for twigs, grass, fur, and leaves.
- Spiders: Research how spiders spin webs. This tedious and delicate process often results in beautiful webs.

Have each student choose one of the above animals or another you have researched and make a thumbprint picture of it using a stamp pad and markers. When the student's picture is complete, have him write and complete the following sentence: "I show perseverance like a (name of animal) by...."

Reach for the Stars

Materials:

- Star Stationery (page 66)
- pencils
- crayons

Ask students if they have ever heard the phrase "Reach for the Stars." Ask them what they think this phrase means. Give each child a copy of the Star Stationery and have her write a paragraph about something she has had to use perseverance to accomplish (riding a bicycle, tying her shoes, roller skating, playing basketball, handwriting, reading a long book, etc.). You may want to have students color their papers, then display them on a class bulletin board or in a class book.

"Reach for the Stars" Magnets

Materials:

- Star pattern (page 67)
- poster board or tagboard
- magnetic tape
- photograph or drawn picture of each student
- glitter
- glue
- scissors
- markers

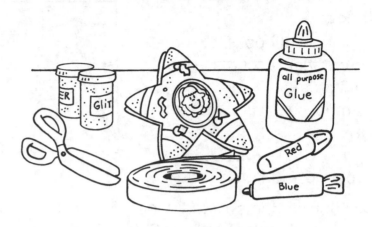

Show students how magnets stick to certain surfaces and not others. Compare magnets with people who stick with an activity. Make two copies of the star pattern on poster board or tagboard for each child. Cut out the stars and cut out a circle in the middle of one of the stars. Have each child decorate her star frame (the one with the cutout circle) using markers and glitter. Place a picture of the child between the frame and the second star. Use glue to secure the two pieces together. Attach a piece of magnetic tape to the back of the frame. Let the children take home their magnets to place on their refrigerators. This should be a reminder to "stick" to their goals while they "reach for the stars!"

Hares and Tortoises

Share the fable of the Hare and the Tortoise with the class (see Literature Selections, page 58). Divide the class into two groups, the Hares and the Tortoises. Have each student write a sentence from the point of view of his character before the race and after the race. Younger students can do this as a group with the teacher writing the sentences on the board. You may also want to have students rewrite the fable to describe what might have happened if the tortoise had not persevered until the end of the race.

"Go for the Goal" Bulletin Board

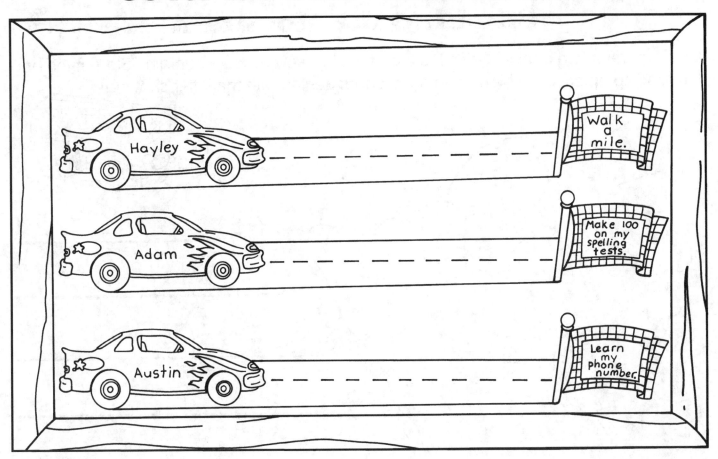

Help each child set a goal for himself that can be accomplished during the unit. Examples include learning multiplication facts, making perfect scores on spelling tests, making a hit in each softball game, etc. Enlarge a copy of the car and flag patterns on page 67 for each child. Have her write her name on the car and then write her goal on the flag. The students should cut out their cars and flags.

Cover the bulletin board with black background paper. Divide the board with white strips of paper or white chalk lines to make race lanes, one for each student (you may need to do several columns of short lanes across your bulletin board). Let students use thumbtacks to place the cars at the beginning of the lanes and the flags at the end. The children can move their cars along the lanes as they get closer to their goals. Reward the children once they have achieved their goals!

Suggested Captions:

- Go for the Goal
- Ready, Set, Go!
- Look Who's Winning
- Running the Race
- Perseverance Pays Off

Name _____

Climbing the Mountain

Help the mountain climber reach the top of the "Perseverance Mountain." Start at the bottom and complete each blank with a word that begins with the letter shown.

E _____

C _____

N _____

A _____

R _____

E _____

V _____

E _____

S _____

R _____

E _____

P _____

Perseverance

Perseverance Critical Thinking

Read the following story to the class. Have the children respond to the questions below for discussion.

Karen and Jane decided they would try out for the girls' basketball team. Both of the girls, however, knew that they needed to work hard to improve their basketball skills. Jane went to the gym one day to practice. After five minutes, Jane became frustrated and tired. Even though she really wanted to play basketball for the team, she did not want to practice or learn to play better. Jane gave up on being on the basketball team.

Jane called Karen and asked her to go to the movies. Karen said "no" because her dad was going to help her with her dribbling. Karen spent three weeks working out in the gym and practicing basketball with her father. After the tryouts, Karen was excited because she was chosen for the team. She felt good about herself because she stuck to her goal of being a better basketball player.

1. Who showed perseverance, Karen or Jane? How?

2. Why do you think Jane gave up on making the team?

3. What was Karen's goal? How did she reach her goal?

4. How do you think Jane feels about Karen making the team?

5. What would you do if you were Jane to try and make the team next year?

Perseverance

Star Stationery

Perseverance Patterns

STAR MOTORS RACING

Respect

What Is Respect?

- Respect is treating others as you would like to be treated.
- Respect is being considerate of other people's feelings.
- Respect means recognizing the value of people, property, the environment, and yourself.

How Can I Show Respect?

Respect is treating others the way that you would like to be treated. When you respect other people, you show them that you value their feelings. You can do this by playing fair, listening, and asking before borrowing something. When you use kind words such as "please" and "thank you," you are showing respect. If you use a borrowed item carefully and return it to its owner, you are also showing respect.

You can also show respect for other people by accepting their differences. A respectful person knows that no two people are alike and he accepts the differences between himself and others. If someone looks different, talks differently, walks differently, or believes something different from you, you show respect by accepting the person and treating him the way you would want to be treated.

It is important that you show respect for yourself with healthy habits. You can take care of your body by eating good foods, brushing your teeth, and exercising. You can take care of your mind by reading, doing your homework, and learning new things.

Animals, the environment, and natural resources also deserve respect. By helping to keep the outdoors clean, you are respecting the homes of wild animals. If you avoid wasting resources, you are showing respect for the environment and for others who may need those resources.

> **Respect means caring and treating others with kindness. By showing respect for others, property, the environment, and yourself, you will, in turn, earn the respect that you deserve!**

📖 Literature Selections

- **Badger's Bring Something Party** by Hiawyn Oram (Lothrop, Lee & Shepard, 1995)
- **Big, Bad Bruce** by Bill Peet (Houghton Mifflin Co., 1977)
- **I Like Me!** by Nancy Carlson (Viking Press, 1988)
- **Kylie's Song** by Patty Sheehan (Advocacy Press, 1988)
- **My Way Sally** by Penelope Paine & Mindy Bingham (Advocacy Press, 1988)
- **The Great Kapok Tree** by Lynne Cherry (Harcourt Brace, 1990)
- **The Ugly Duckling** by Hans Christian Andersen (Andrews and McMeel Publishers, 1992)

Song of Respect

Materials:
- chart paper and marker

Write the words to the following song on chart paper and teach children one verse each day. After students have mastered the song, younger children might enjoy making up hand motions while older children could add their own verses.

Song:

Sing to the tune of "He's Got the Whole World in His Hands."

I have respect for you and me,
It can be easy, you will see.
Have respect for the things you see,
Others, self, and property.

I have respect for you and me.
I show other people the best in me.
I respect my friends and teachers too.
It is the proper thing to do.

I have respect for you and me.
I take care of others' property.
I respect the earth and the animals too.
Respect in everything I do.

I have respect for you and me.
It can be easy, you will see.
Have respect for the things you see:
Others, self, and property.

Respect Your School

Discuss the importance of respecting classroom and school property. Have the students look around the classroom and then around the school to point out areas where respectful behavior was used (i.e., a recycling station). Have the students also point out areas where respectful behavior may not have been used (for example, trash on the ground instead of in a wastebasket). Ask the students why it is important to show respect to classroom and school property (to keep it safe and pleasant, to show teachers and other students that you care about the property you share, etc.).

After your discussion, return to the areas in the school where respectful behavior may not have been used. Ask the students what they can do to "correct" the situations, and then allow them to put their plans into action. You might have the class write a "thank-you" note to another class or to a school employee who was responsible for one of the areas where respectful behavior was used.

Put Trash in its Place

Respect Our Differences

One aspect of respect is showing understanding and acceptance of differences. Divide the class into pairs. Direct each pair of students to talk for a few moments and find out three things that are the same about the two of them and three things that are different. After all of the pairs have finished, reassemble the class to share their findings. As an extension, have the class brainstorm the similarities and differences between boys and girls, young and old people, people born in your country and people born elsewhere, physically challenged people and those who are not physically challenged, etc.

Manners = Respect

Materials:

- Situation Cards (page 76)
- small paper or cloth bag
- chart paper and marker
- scissors

Ask students how showing good manners is a way of showing respect to others. Hang a large sheet of chart paper with the words "Good Manners" written at the top. Ask the children to tell you what they think good manners are and let them list special "good manners words" that they can use (i.e., "please," "thank you, "excuse me," etc.). Write their responses on the chart. Reproduce and cut out the situation cards and place them in a small paper or cloth bag. Call on individuals to pull situations from the bag and role-play the scenes using good manners.

Nicknames of Respect

Materials:

- 5" construction paper circles, one per student
- hole punch
- yarn
- markers or crayons

Ask the children if anyone has a nickname. Explain that sometimes our parents or friends call us by nicknames, but that it is not respectful to call someone a name that is hurtful or unkind. Have the students think up nice nicknames for themselves. Each student should think of a word that begins with the first letter of his name and reminds him of respectful behavior (for example, "Kind Kelly," "Helpful Hayley," "Attentive Adam," etc.). This can be the student's new "Nickname of Respect."

Have each student write his respectful nickname on a paper circle and decorate the circle using markers or crayons. Punch a hole at the top of the circle and thread a length of yarn through the hole. Tie the yarn to make a necklace. Allow the students to wear their name tags throughout the week.

70

Respect Collages

Materials:

- old magazines and catalogs
- construction paper
- glue
- scissors

Make "Everyone Deserves Respect" Collages with the students. Have the students look through old magazines and catalogs for pictures of all kinds of people. Direct the students to cut out the pictures and glue them onto construction paper. When the collages are finished, invite each student to tell about his collage and how to respect the differences in people. Display the collages on a bulletin board or in a class book during your discussion on respect.

Recycle for Respect!

Materials:

- clean plastic soda bottles, milk jugs, egg cartons, newspaper, cans, and other materials for use in art projects
- construction paper, paint, glue, scissors, and other craft materials

Review with the students the importance of showing respect for the environment. Make sure they understand that one way people can show respect for the environment is by recycling. Have the students brainstorm a list of materials that can be recycled. You might even want the class to make a graph of the different materials students recycle at home. Then, allow the students to make "recycled art," such as a planter from an old milk carton. Provide potting soil and small rooted plants for the students to plant. Have the students decorate the outside of their planters with paint, if desired. Other recycled art projects students might choose:

- terrariums made from plastic soda bottles
- banks made from milk jugs
- papier mâché creatures made from newspaper
- wrapping paper made from newspaper scraps
- pencil holders made from cans

Golden Rule

Materials:

- 12" x 12" piece of poster board for each child
- markers
- glue
- gold glitter

Ask your students if anyone has ever heard of the "Golden Rule." If possible, have a student share with the others in the class what the Golden Rule is: Do unto others as you would have them do unto you. Ask the students what they think the Golden Rule means. Discuss how the Golden Rule was written a long time ago as a reminder to always show respect.

Allow the children to make their own signs displaying the Golden Rule. Give each child a 12" x 12" piece of poster board. Have the student write, "Do unto others as you would have them do unto you," on the poster board with markers. Then, have each child carefully squeeze a thin line of glue around the poster board so that it resembles a picture frame. Have the children sprinkle gold glitter on top of the glue. After a few moments, have each child gently shake his picture over a trash can to remove any excess glitter. Allow the glue to dry and then encourage the students to take their posters home and display them. Be sure to make a classroom copy of the Golden Rule as a reminder for respectful behavior at school.

Respect Rules

Materials:

- chart paper or poster board and marker
- gold foil stickers
- gold foil-wrapped candy, optional

After your discussion of the Golden Rule and what it means (see activity above), have the children brainstorm ways that they would like to be treated at school. Then, have them turn their ideas into rules for treating others at school. Be sure that positive behaviors such as listening to others, keeping unkind thoughts to themselves, playing fairly and taking turns, raising hands when wanting to speak, saying kind words, and cleaning up after themselves are mentioned in the discussion. Write the students' rules for respectful behavior on a chart or poster and display it in your classroom. On another piece of chart paper or poster board, list the names of the students. Every time you see a student showing one of the respectful behaviors, place a gold star beside her name. If desired, as each student earns a predetermined number of stickers, reward her with a gold foil-wrapped piece of candy.

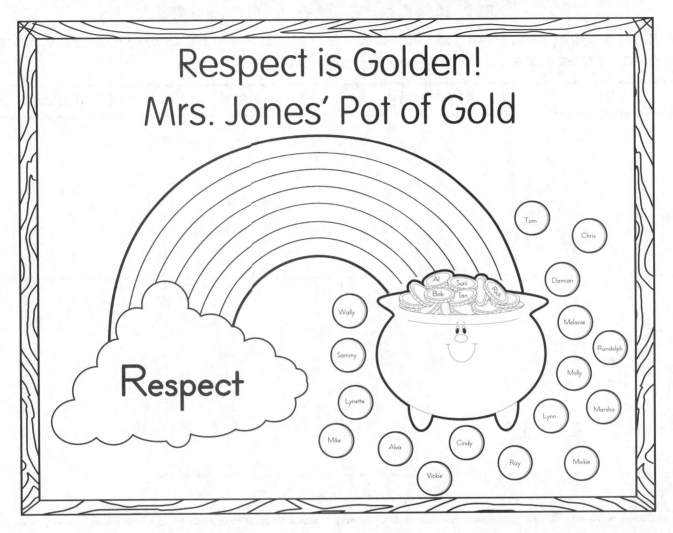

Cover the bulletin board with blue background paper to represent the sky, then add green paper to represent the ground. Enlarge the Cloud pattern from page 77 and the Pot of Gold pattern from page 78 and place them at opposite ends of the board. Color or paint a rainbow with seven bands between the cloud and pot. If desired, cut out letters or use a letter-cutter to make letters for words such as "Self," "Others," "Property," "Environment," etc. Attach these letters to the rainbow with thumbtacks, glue, or tape. Title the bulletin board, "Respect is Golden! (Teacher's name)'s Pot of Gold." Give each child a coin pattern from page 77. Let each child write her name on the coin and place the coin around the pot on the bulletin board.

Name _____

Cut and Paste Respect

Cut out the eight squares at the bottom of the page. Paste each activity to show whether it demonstrates respect to self, property, others, or environment.

Self	Property	Others	Environment

Return library books on time.	Exercise.	Put things back where they belong.	Pick up litter.
Share toys.	Recycle.	Eat healthy food.	Take turns.

Critical Thinking Activity

Read the following story to the class. Use the questions below in class discussion.

Misao has just moved to town from Japan. She is excited about being at a new school. When Misao comes to school, all the other students stare at her because she is new and because she looks different.

On the way to class, Misao hears some of the other boys and girls talking about her. They stop talking and walk away when they see her.

At lunch time, the other children notice that Misao is eating with chopsticks. She uses them as well as the other children use forks. Some of the boys and girls ask Misao about the chopsticks and she tells them that many people in Japan eat with chopsticks.

The next day, Misao brings chopsticks for everyone in her class. The boys and girls try them at lunch and realize that eating with them takes practice. When lunch is over, the teacher reads a book about Japan to the class. Afterwards, the boys and girls let Misao know they are happy to have her in their class.

1. How do you think Misao felt going to her new school?

2. How would you feel about moving to a new country?

3. Have you ever been the new student somewhere? How did you feel about being new?

4. What do you think the boys and girls might have been saying about Misao?

5. Did the other children show respect for Misao at first? How do you know?

6. How do you think Misao feels about her class now?

7. What did the boys and girls do to show Misao they respected her?

8. What are some other ways we can show respect for others?

Respect Situation Cards

You would like to have a drink of water.	You accidentally step on your friend's foot.
Your aunt brings you a present.	You see someone who looks different from you.
Your mother is talking on the phone and you want to ask her a question.	You sneeze.
You are standing in line for lunch.	Your teacher asks the class a question and you know the answer.
You would like the mashed potatoes but the bowl is on the other side of the table.	You finish your work before the other students in the class.
You are angry because your father will not let you buy a candy bar.	Your new classmate has to use a wheelchair.
You are finished with your picnic, but the trash can is at the other side of the park.	You and your sister want to listen to different radio stations.
Your dog's water dish is empty, but your favorite TV show is about to come on.	Your grandmother calls to you from another room.

Respect

Respect Patterns

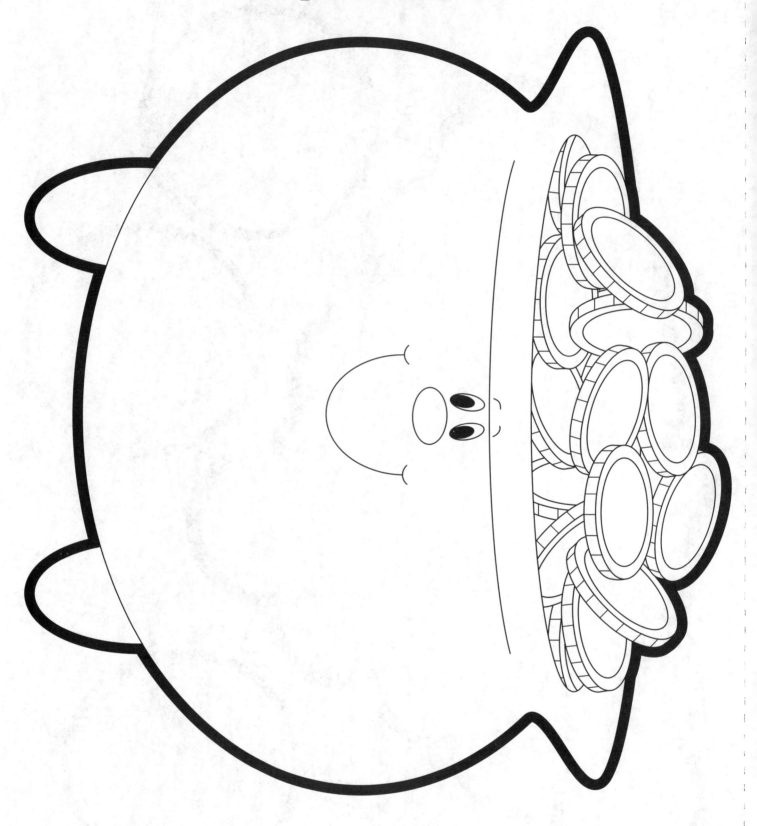

Responsibility

What Is Responsibility?

- Responsibility is being dependable and accountable for your words and actions.
- Responsibility is also doing your best and never blaming others for your mistakes.
- Being responsible for a job means that you are the one who makes sure it is done correctly and on time.

How Can I Show Responsibility?

When you show that you are dependable, you show responsibility. When you tell someone you will do something, that person is counting on you to "pull your weight." When you do a good job and finish on time, you are showing that you are responsible. A responsible person always does his best, and does not blame others for his mistakes.

You also show responsibility by the choices you make. Every day, you make many decisions which affect your life. Some choices are small, such as choosing what to wear to school or what to eat for lunch. Some decisions, such as the way you treat others and do your chores, affect other people. When you make appropriate choices, you are showing others you are responsible.

You can be responsible by taking care of your possessions. You should take care of your school supplies, library books, and money. If you own a pet, it is counting on you to feed it, provide water, give it exercise, and keep it clean. When you do these things, you show responsibility.

We also count on other people to be responsible. Imagine what the world would be like if no one took responsibility for taking out trash or cleaning up messes. You count on others to be responsible, just as others count on you.

> A responsible person knows that he has many jobs to do and often others are counting on him to get the job done. When you try your best and work hard to do what you are supposed to do, you show responsibility.

📖 Literature Selections

- **Airmail to the Moon** by Tom Birdseye (Holiday House, 1988)
- **Arthur's Computer Disaster** by Marc Brown (Little, Brown & Co., 1997))
- **Dogger** by Shirley Hughes (Lothrop, Lee & Shepard, 1988)
- **It's Up to You, Griffin** by Susan T. Pickford and Mary Dunn Ramsey (Tidewater Publishing, 1993)
- **The Berenstain Bears and the Blame Game** by Stan and Jan Berenstain (Random House, 1997)
- **The Little Red Hen** by Paul Galdone (Houghton Mifflin, 1985)

Responsibility Project

Materials:

- paper and pencils
- crayons or markers
- any materials necessary to complete chosen group project

As a class, decide on a group project for which the students would like to be responsible. Discuss ideas such as these:

- tutoring students in lower grades or another class
- picking up litter on school grounds
- decorating a prominent school bulletin board
- providing food for a homeless shelter
- providing refreshments at a PTA meeting
- becoming pen-pals with residents of a nursing home
- planting a school garden and taking care of it
- adopting a class pet (guinea pig, fish, etc.)

Make sure every student has an opportunity to show responsibility during the project. After the students have completed the task, have each student draw a picture of the "responsibility project" and write a sentence or two about how he was responsible. Display student work on a bulletin board or combine it into a class book.

School Responsibilities

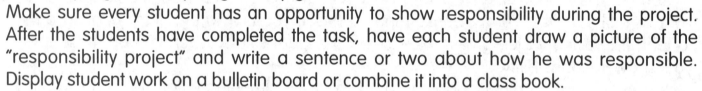

Materials:

- camera and film, or disposable camera
- chart paper and marker
- paper and pencils

Discuss the responsibilities of various people who work at your school. These could include the principal, secretary, custodian, cafeteria staff, teachers, assistants, librarian, bus drivers, guidance counselor, and students. Make a chart showing each person's title, then have students list specific responsibilities of the job and consequences if the job is not done. Allow the students to use a camera to take photographs of the various workers. Have each child choose one of the workers and write a few sentences about her responsibilities at the school. Display the students' writing on a bulletin board or in a class book along with the photographs. If desired, have the class write thank-you notes to the workers.

Cooperative Cooking

Materials:

- ingredients for a simple recipe, such as cookies, cupcakes, or muffins
- measuring cups and spoons
- mixing bowl
- spoon
- baking pan appropriate for the recipe you are making
- oven

Use a simple recipe as a way to reinforce the importance of everyone fulfilling their responsibilities. Divide the students into small groups. Assign each group a responsibility from the list below:

- reading the recipe
- measuring the ingredients
- stirring the mixture
- turning on the oven
- timing the cooking
- dividing the finished product among the students
- cleaning up

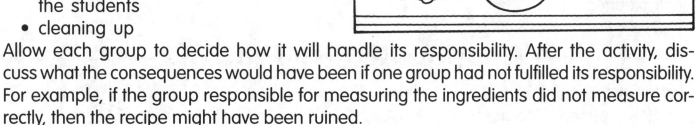

Allow each group to decide how it will handle its responsibility. After the activity, discuss what the consequences would have been if one group had not fulfilled its responsibility. For example, if the group responsible for measuring the ingredients did not measure correctly, then the recipe might have been ruined.

Healthy Responsibility

Materials:

- white construction paper
- crayons or markers
- scissors
- stapler

Talk with the children about taking responsibility for their health. Explain that eating healthy foods, exercising, and brushing their teeth daily are just a few ways people can be responsible for their health. Have each child create a "Healthy Me" booklet. Give each child four small pieces of white construction paper, approximately 4" x 4", stapled together to form a small booklet. Have her write "Healthy Me" on the cover and decorate it using markers or crayons. Then, have her illustrate a healthy activity on each of the remaining pages. Have the student dictate or write a sentence describing each illustration. Place the booklets in an area where the class can read and share them.

Responsibility Pledge

Materials:
- Responsibility Pledge letter (page 88)
- I'm Responsible bracelet patterns (page 89)
- construction paper, cut into 1" strips
- crayons or markers
- scissors
- tape

Reproduce a Responsibility Pledge letter for each student. Have the student complete the letter with a task for which he will be responsible at home. Explain that the students must complete their tasks each day for seven days in a row. Send the letter home with the student and ask that it be returned on the specified date. When the students return the completed letters to school, present those who upheld their pledges with "I'm Responsible" bracelet patterns to color, cut out, and wear. Let each child tape her pattern to the center of a construction paper strip and then tape the completed Responsibility Bracelet around her wrist. Let the students wear their bracelets throughout the day to show that they upheld their pledges.

Responsibility Flowers

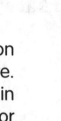

Materials:
- Petal patterns (page 89)
- small paper plates
- extra-long craft sticks
- yellow paper
- green construction paper
- glue
- pencils, crayons, or markers
- scissors

For each child, make eight copies of the Petal pattern on yellow paper. Provide each child with a small paper plate. Instruct her to write the sentence, "I am responsible," in the middle of the plate. Have her write something for which she is responsible on each petal. (Responsibilities might include picking up toys, cleaning up her room, feeding her pet, turning in her homework, etc.) After the child has written a responsibility on each petal, let her cut out and glue the petals around the paper plate "flower." Provide each child with an extra-long craft stick, glue, and green construction paper. Have the child glue the craft stick onto the back of the paper plate to represent a stem. Then, have the child cut out two or three leaves from the green construction paper and glue the leaves onto the craft stick stem. Display the responsibility flowers around your classroom.

School Supply Kits

Materials:

- shoe box with lid, one for each student
- stickers, sequins, glitter, and other decorative materials
- decorative paper, such as gift wrap or wallpaper
- clear tape
- markers
- glue
- scissors

Encourage students to be responsible for their school supplies by making "school supply kits." Before beginning, discuss with students what might happen if they were not responsible with their school tools, books, homework, and school property. Explain that they are going to make their own boxes to help keep their supplies safe and accessible.

Give each student a shoe box with a lid. Have her cover it with decorative paper. Then, let her decorate it using craft materials. Make sure she writes her name on the box.

Pick a location for the students to store their boxes. Encourage them to place their pencils, crayons, scissors, glue, etc., in their boxes so the materials can be safe and easy to find when they are needed.

Field Trip

Visit the local public library. Ask a librarian if she could discuss with students how the library system is set up and who is eligible to borrow books. Have her explain the responsibilities of every library patron to take care of the materials borrowed and return them on time so that others may borrow them too. Discuss with the students how the library system is built on trust and responsibility, two very important character traits. If possible, have the library issue each child his own library card and allow him to borrow a book and return it on time.

Responsibility Writing

Materials:

- chart paper and marker
- writing paper and pencils

Write the following "letter" (or one similar) on a large piece of chart paper and sign it. Provide each student with paper to write a letter explaining why he is a good choice for this responsibility.

Example letter:

> Dear Students,
>   I am looking for a student who can be responsible for taking up lunch money. Please write me a letter telling me why you are the right person for the job, and how you will show responsibility with this task.

When the students have completed their letters, allow them to share their writing with the class. Then, let each child have a turn at showing responsibility by completing the chosen task.

Responsibility Venn Diagram

Materials:

- chalkboard and chalk or chart paper and marker

As a class, make a list of things to consider when you are responsible for a dog. Examples: a dog needs water, sun, food, and exercise. A dog can be messy. A dog can make a lot of noise. A dog can play with you.

Next, make a list of things to consider when you are responsible for a plant. Examples: a plant needs water, sun, and soil. A plant is not messy. A plant is quiet. A plant is pretty.

Create a Venn Diagram based on the results by putting all things exclusive to a dog in one circle and all things exclusive to a plant in the other. Where the circles overlap, write the things which the two have in common.

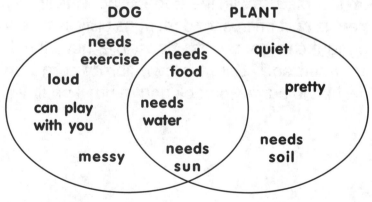

Other comparisons for use in diagramming might include home versus school responsibilities or responsibilities of teacher and student. You may want to encourage older students to complete their own Venn diagrams using a model.

Have the children name things for which they are responsible at school. List the items on a piece of chart paper or on the chalkboard. Then, give each child a copy of the speech balloon and torso patterns on page 90. Have him draw facial features, add hair using yarn or construction paper strips, and draw clothes using crayons or markers. Have the child write or dictate one of his school responsibilities in the speech balloon. For example, "I feed Snowball, the rabbit," or "I clean the chalkboards." Display each pattern and the accompanying speech balloon on the bulletin board. Title the display, "(Teacher name)'s Class Gets the Job Done."

Are They Responsible?

Read each sentence. Circle "YES" if the person showed responsibility. Circle "NO" if the person did not show responsibility.

1. Mary picked up her toys when she was finished playing with them.   YES   NO

2. Jordan helped his dad fix dinner.   YES   NO

3. Louis forgot to feed his dog before going to play.   YES   NO

4. Tara cleaned up her room every day.   YES   NO

5. Robert only brushed his teeth when his mother told him to.   YES   NO

6. Paul took the trash cans to the curb on trash day.   YES   NO

7. Mark missed the school bus because he was busy playing a video game.   YES   NO

8. Kim left her homework at home.   YES   NO

9. William returned the books he borrowed to the library on time.   YES   NO

10. Nicky completed all of his work at school.   YES   NO

Choose a sentence from above that tells about a person who is not showing responsibility. Rewrite the sentence and draw a picture so the sentence shows responsible behavior.

Note to Teacher: To make this worksheet appropriate for younger children, read the situations aloud and have students give a "thumbs up" or "thumbs down" to indicate whether the subject is showing responsibility or not.

Responsibility   86   © Carson-Dellosa Publ. CD-7318

Critical Thinking Activity

Read the following story to your students. Afterward, use the discussion questions to provide the students with a critical thinking activity.

Mary was a bright and energetic girl with many friends. One day, as she was out playing, her mother called to her. She asked Mary if she would watch her younger brother, Zack, while she went to the store. Mary said, "OK, Mom!" as she came running into the house.

Right after Mom left for the store, Mary's friend Christy called. Christy told Mary that she and two other friends wanted to come over and listen to Mary's new compact discs. Mary knew that her mother did not allow friends to visit without first asking permission, but she really wanted to see her friends. She said, "Sure, come on over!"

When the friends arrived, the four girls ran into the kitchen to grab soda, cookies, and chips and then went to Mary's room. They shut the door and started listening to the CDs, dancing, and eating their snacks.

Mary's mom came home from the store and heard the loud music coming from Mary's room. She knocked on the door. When Mary opened the door, her mother could not believe her eyes! Food and soda were everywhere! Mary's CDs were thrown all around the room, as were her bedspread, school books, and clothes.

Then, Mary's Mom asked, "Where is your brother?" Oh, no! Mary had forgotten all about taking care of Zack! Where was he? Mary's mother and the four girls ran through the house shouting, "Zack, where are you?"

Suddenly the doorbell rang. It was the next door neighbor, Mrs. Cranford. Zack had walked down the street to her house and he was crying for his mother. Luckily, he was safe. Mary knew, by the look on her mom's face, that she had not been a very responsible person that day.

1. What responsibility did Mary's mom give her?

2. How would you have handled this type of responsibility?

3. Was Mary showing responsibility when she allowed her friends to come over and play? Why or why not?

4. What kind of irresponsible behavior did the girls show in Mary's room?

5. How do you think Zack felt as he was walking down the street crying for his mother?

6. Why was Mary's mother disappointed in her?

7. What could Mary have done differently to act responsibly?

8. What can Mary do to show her mother that she can act responsibly?

Responsibility Pledge

Date _____

Dear Parents,

    Our class has been learning about responsibility. Your child has pledged that he or she will be responsible for a task at home. Each day that your child shows responsibility with this task, please write the date with your initials.

Please return this sheet by _____ . Thank you.

Sincerely,

_____

Child's name: _____

Responsibility: _____

Student signature: _____

Date						
Parent Initials						

Responsibility Patterns

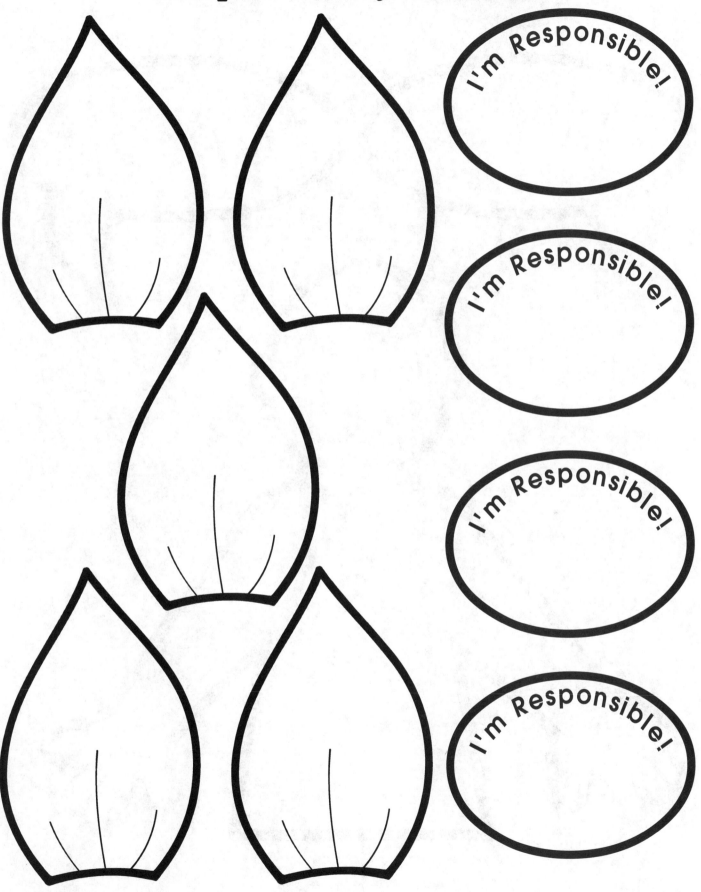

Responsibility Patterns

Self-Discipline

What Is Self-Discipline?

- Self-discipline is making good choices.
- Self-discipline is having control over your thoughts and actions.
- Self-discipline includes practicing good habits, being patient, controlling your temper, and taking responsibility for your actions.

How Can I Show Self-Discipline?

A self-disciplined person thinks before he acts. If something is unkind or not the right thing to do, a self-disciplined person has the control not to do it.

You can show good self-discipline by having good health habits, such as brushing your teeth, combing your hair, washing your face and hands, and eating healthy foods each day. Taking good care of yourself is showing self-discipline.

Self-discipline is a character trait that is important to demonstrate at school as well. By completing your assignments, waiting to be called on before speaking, making good choices, and doing what you think is right, you are showing self-discipline.

Because your actions can affect those around you, it is important to show self-discipline when you are with others. Keeping your hands to yourself and controlling your temper when things do not go your way are two examples of showing self-discipline around others.

> **Being self-disciplined means being responsible for yourself. This means that you are in charge of all the things you say and do. You could call it your "self-control." When you are in control, you can make choices that are healthy, safe, kind, and respectful to others.**

📖 Literature Selections

- **Alexander, Who Used to Be Rich Last Sunday** by Judith Viorst (Simon & Schuster, 1980)
- **Farmer Duck** by Martin Waddell (Candlewick Press, 1991)
- **Hey, Al** by Arthur Yorinks (Farrar, Strauss & Giroux, 1986)
- **Lilly's Purple Plastic Purse** by Kevin Henkes (Greenwillow Books, 1996)
- **Princess Prunella and the Purple Peanut** by Margaret Atwood (Workman Publishing Company, 1995)
- **The Berenstain Bears and the Homework Hassle** by Stan and Jan Berenstain (Random House, 1997)

Self Portraits

Materials:

- white paper
- crayons and markers
- mirrors

Discuss with your students the fact that the word self-discipline—and the character trait itself—begins with "self." Being self-disciplined is not something that a parent, teacher, or friend can do for you. Only one's self can be in control of behavior.

If possible, provide each student with a small mirror. If this is not possible, have one large mirror available. Allow the students to look at their "selves" in the mirrors. Provide paper and markers for the students to draw "self" portraits.

Replace a Bad Habit with a Good One

Materials:

- Watch Me Succeed card (page 100)
- newsprint cut in 1" x 4" pieces
- large rock
- tape
- shovel
- paint pen or permanent marker
- pencils

Discuss with your class how each of us has different habits. A habit is the way we go about doing something time after time. The kinds of habits one has tell a lot about that person's self-discipline. Examples would be how often you brush your teeth and wash your hands, how you pack your school bag, if you raise your hand before talking in class, if you say "please" and "thank-you," and whether you interrupt others when they are talking.

Next, talk about changing bad habits into good habits. Hand out the strips of newsprint and ask each child to write one of her bad habits on the strip. If desired, allow each child to share her bad habit with the group, tell why she wants to change it, and tell what habit she wants in its place. (Note: If a student is uncomfortable sharing her bad habit, let her know she does not have to share it.)

Take the class outside. Choose a good place to dig a hole and bury all the bad habits together. Explain that just as it takes time for the newsprint to become a part of the earth that can then grow good things, it will take time to make the new habits permanent (teaching patience). Use a rock to mark the burial spot and have children sign the rock with a paint pen or permanent marker.

Return to the classroom and give each child a copy of the Watch Me Succeed card. Have children write their new habits on the cards, then color the borders and tape the cards to their desks.

In two or three weeks, ask students how well they are doing with their new habits. As new habits are established, bring the painted rock inside and plant flowers in its place.

Role Playing

Materials:
- Self-Discipline Situation Cards (page 100)
- container such as a bowl, box, or basket
- chart paper and marker

Reproduce the Self-Discipline Situation Cards onto heavy paper and cut them apart. Place the cards in a container and mix them. Divide the class into small groups or pairs and ask each group to choose a situation from the container (an adult could read it to smaller children). Allow students some time to quietly discuss what they will do to role play their situation.

As each group acts out its situation, the rest of the class tells ways the characters could show more self-discipline. The suggestions for improvement can be recorded on large chart paper. Continue to display the suggestions so you can refer to them as you encourage self-discipline daily in your classroom.

As a follow up activity, students could role play the situations again, but with the characters showing self-discipline.

In-Control Patrol

Materials:
- chart paper
- small slips of paper
- container such as bowl, basket, or small box
- marker

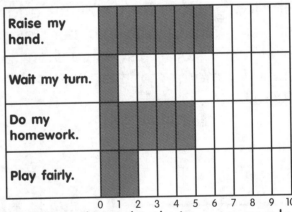

As a class, brainstorm ways that children can show self-discipline at school. Write down all the ideas that the class can generate in two or three minutes.

Remind students that good self-discipline is shown when the right choices are made and when someone is in control of his thoughts and behavior. Ask each student to write on a small slip of paper one of the ways that he shows self-discipline at school. Have the children place their slips into a container. Read the responses from the class and sort them into categories that show same or similar responses.

On a sheet of chart paper, make a graph showing all the categories of responses. Have the students count together the number of responses in each category. Graph the results.

Award each student a special treat when he demonstrates one of the ways to show self-discipline at school.

In-Control Patrol Vest

Materials:
- large paper grocery bags
- crayons or markers
- scissors

Before the activity, cut the grocery bags into vest shapes, following the diagram shown. During class, talk about self-discipline in your classroom and review class rules. Give each child a vest. Ask him to write three characteristics of a person who has good self-discipline on the back of his vest in dark crayon or marker.

Just as football players earn stars on their helmets for good plays, members of the "In-Control Patrol" can earn awards for good self-discipline in your classroom. When a student demonstrates good self-discipline, add a sticker, a stamp (with a rubber stamp), or a paper star to his vest to show that he is a membr of the "In-Control" Patrol!

Think Before You Act

Materials:
- chalkboard and chalk
- chart paper and marker, optional

Write the phrase, "Think before you act," on the board. Ask the students if they can tell you what they think this phrase means. Discuss how often people make bad choices with words or actions because they have not really thought about the consequences of the bad behavior. Allow the students to practice this concept by asking questions, or having them ask themselves questions like, "Is it kind? Is it safe? Is it healthy? Is it the right thing to do?" You may want to display these questions on a chart in your classroom as an everyday reminder.

Visit from a Farmer

Materials:

- list of approximately five tasks to be completed (one copy per child)

Invite a farmer from a working farm in your area to visit your class and help students learn about time management. Brainstorm ahead of time to have students think about a farmer's job. Ask students questions like these: What kind of self-discipline do you think a farmer might need to have? How will you be able to tell if the farmer has self-discipline?

Make sure students ask the farmer many "when" and "what time" questions to get a sense of a farmer's schedule (i.e., how early he has to rise, planting and harvesting deadlines he must meet, etc.).

After the visit, give students a list of tasks they must complete in a certain amount of time. Make sure the activities are age-appropriate and can be completed within the given time, but do make them challenging to accomplish. Discuss how it will take self-discipline and time management to complete all the tasks in the given amount of time. A task list might include sharpening a pencil, reading a book, completing a puzzle, washing hands, etc.

Lilly's Mail

Materials:

- book, **Lilly's Purple Plastic Purse** by Kevin Henkes (Greenwillow Books, 1996)
- paper
- letter-sized envelopes, optional
- pencils
- box or basket

Share the story of **Lilly's Purple Plastic Purse** with students. Lilly is a mouse who learns a lesson about impatience and angry deeds. After reading the story, tell students you would like for each of them to give Lilly some advice by writing her a letter. (Younger children could dictate a group letter.) Tell the children to include ways that Lilly can improve her behavior, things not to do again, how people might feel when she acts as she does, and a compliment for something she did well. If desired, have students fold the letters and put them in envelopes. Collect them in a box or basket labeled "Lilly's Mail."

Share the letters by having everyone select one from the basket to read aloud. Students might also enjoy writing responses from Lilly.

Stay in Control

A fun way to practice self-discipline and staying in control is to play "Simon Says." Tell the class to obey only the instructions which have the command "Simon says" before them. Give various instructions with and without stating "Simon says" first. The students can be told to stand on one foot, clap their hands, flap their arms, touch the floor, etc. Those who do the activity without the preface of "Simon says" must sit out until the next game. Continue until only one student is left.

Afterward, have the students discuss how they had to use self-discipline to stay in control of their listening, movement, etc.

Healthy Choices Place Mat

Materials:

- construction paper
- old magazines
- laminator or clear adhesive paper
- crayons or markers
- glue
- scissors

Discuss with students the importance of showing self-discipline with food choices. While another cupcake or piece of candy may be tempting, a self-disciplined person knows when to say "no" to too much junk food. By making healthy food choices, a person is showing good self-discipline.

Give each student a sheet of construction paper. Direct students to write the words "Healthy Food Choices" on their paper. Then, instruct them to look through magazines and cut out pictures of healthy food choices. Have them glue the pictures to the construction paper. You might want the children to also draw a few pictures of healthy foods to make the place mats more original. Laminate or cover the place mats with clear adhesive paper.

Use this bulletin board to help set goals for new self-discipline behaviors. Enlarge a copy of one of the soccer ball patterns from page 102 for each student. Have students write self-discipline goals on their soccer balls. Examples of goals include: "I will wait until I'm called on before talking."; "I will not hit my brother when I am angry with him."; "I will practice soccer for 30 minutes every day."

Cover the bulletin board with green paper to represent grass. Using yarn or string, make a "soccer goal" at one end of the board or use the net pattern from page 101. Enlarge the soccer player pattern from page 101 and place it on the other side of the board. Attach the students' completed soccer ball patterns to the finish the display.

Suggested Headings:
- Goals for Self-Discipline
- We're Off To A Great Start
- Watch Us Score Goals in (Teacher name)'s Class
- Kickoff for Self-Discipline

Self-Discipline

Name _____

What's Wrong with this Picture?

For each scene, rewrite what is said so the person will be showing good self-discipline.

"I'll feed the fish for the whole week today. It will save time."

_____

_____

_____

"If I run to the classroom door, I can be first in line."

_____

_____

_____

"What a great lunch: chips, a candy bar, and a soda!"

_____

_____

_____

"It's okay to come to school late since I stayed up so late last night."

_____

_____

_____

Note to teacher: Older students may write their answers on the lines. For younger students, you may want to discuss the situations as a class or have students draw pictures that show good self-discipline.

Critical Thinking Activity

Share the following story with students, then use the questions below in a class discussion.

Frank's mother was in a panic! She was having eight guests for dinner and she suddenly realized that she did not have a dessert to serve. She asked Frank to take $5.00 from her purse and go to the store to buy a pie. Frank took the money and walked to the store. As Frank walked towards the bakery section, he caught a glimpse of a brightly colored toy airplane that was for sale. Frank thought about how fun it would be to have the toy airplane. He looked at the price tag and it said $3.00. He then ran to the bakery where he discovered that a pie also cost $3.00.

Frank knew that he would need $6.00 to buy both the airplane and the pie, and that the $5.00 his mother had given him was not enough. Frank also knew that the right thing to do was to buy the pie for his mother, and perhaps buy the airplane at a later time. As he went to buy the pie, however, Frank could not stop thinking about the airplane. Before he knew it, he was walking out of the store with the toy airplane, $2.00 in change, and no pie. He skipped home, excited about playing with his new toy. As he arrived home, he saw his mother's guests arriving for dinner.

1. Did Frank show self-discipline with the $5.00 his mother gave him? Why or why not?

2. What should Frank have done to stay "in control" of his actions at the store?

3. How have you shown self-discipline with money?

4. What do you think will happen when Frank goes inside and sees his mother?

5. How do you think Frank's mother will feel?

Self-Discipline

Self-Discipline Patterns

Watch Me Succeed
in
My New Good Habits!

_____

_____

_____

_____

Self-Discipline Situation Cards

John whistles while he works in class.	Amy runs to get in line at the classroom door.	Marcus pouts because he can't have his way.
Polly asks a friend for the answer to a test question.	Bart arrives late at school because he stayed up too late.	Misty eats her cupcake first and then is not hungry for anything else.
Andrew falls asleep at his desk.	Cassie won't stop talking during class.	Willie doesn't do his home-work and makes up an excuse.
Lisa interrupts the teacher.	Charles is mad and throws his book.	Lynn fidgets and makes paper airplanes during class.

Self-Discipline Patterns

Self-Discipline

Self-Discipline Patterns

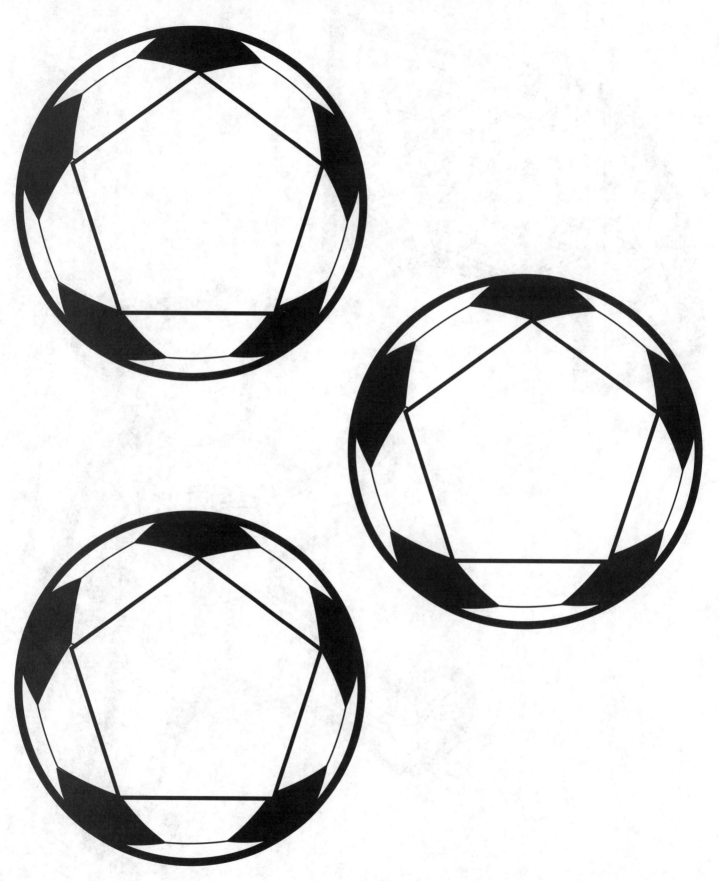

Trustworthiness

What Is Trustworthiness?

- Trustworthiness means being honest with others.
- Trustworthiness means keeping promises.
- Trustworthiness also means others can depend on you and trust you.

How Can I Be Trustworthy?

A trustworthy person is someone you can count on to do what is right. Being trustworthy means that you have earned the trust of other people.

If you are trustworthy, you always do your very best to keep your promises. Other people know they can count on you to do what you say you will do. Being trustworthy means being dependable.

It is also important to know which people you can trust. A trustworthy person is someone you can count on never to intentionally hurt you with unkind words or actions. You can learn to tell which people to trust and which people not to trust.

Some people say that a trustworthy person can "be counted on." This means that you can be sure a trustworthy person will keep his word and do what he says. By keeping promises and being a good friend, you can be a trustworthy person.

📖 Literature Selections

- **Doctor DeSoto** by William Steig (Scholastic, Inc., 1982)
- **Frog and Toad Are Friends** by Arnold Lobel (HarperCollins, Inc., 1970)
- **Horton Hatches an Egg** by Dr. Seuss (Random House Books for Young Readers, 1987)
- **Hurry Up, Franklin!** by Paulette Bourgeois and Brenda Clark (HarperCollins, 1990)
- **Strega Nona** by Tomie de Paola (Simon & Schuster, 1997)
- **The Berenstain Bears and the Truth** by Stan & Jan Berenstain (Scholastic, 1983)

Duty Chart

Materials:
- paper and pencils
- crayons and markers
- gold star stickers, optional

Have each student make a list of five duties that others trust him to do at school, such as taking care of school materials, telling the truth, or doing his own work. Allow the students to make "trustworthy duty charts." Each day, have the students draw a star beside the activities they have completed. If desired, reward students who bring back a completed chart with a gold star sticker.

Adam's Trustworthy Duties

	Mon.	Tues.	Wed.	Thurs.	Fri.
Take care of school materials.	★	★			
Finish my assignments.	★	★			
Tell the truth.	★	★	★		
Keep my promises.	★	★	★		
Play fairly.	★	★	★		

Trustworthy Characters

Share with the class some classic folk and fairy tales that have characters who are or are not trustworthy. An example of a trustworthy character is the spider from "Charlotte's Web." Characters who are not trustworthy include the wolf from "Little Red Riding Hood," Foxy Loxy from "Henny Penny," etc.

After sharing a story, have the class rewrite it, either individually or as a group, to show untrustworthy characters as trustworthy. Have students tell the differences in the way the characters act.

As an extension of this activity, have students identify other folk- and fairytale characters who show trustworthiness.

Community Helpers Prop Box

Materials:

- several items of clothing or tools that relate to different community helpers, such as the following:
    - first aid kit, stethoscope—paramedic, doctor, nurse
    - cardboard police badge, police hat, whistle—police officer
    - boots, small water hose, large overcoat—firefighter
    - books, stamp pad and rubber stamp—librarian
    - envelopes, empty boxes—postal worker
    - tools such as screwdriver, hammer, wrench—construction worker, repair person
- chart paper and marker

Have the children name community helpers that they count on to help them in emergencies. Discuss the fact that many people need these helpers. It is important that they are trustworthy and know how to do their jobs. Allow the children to dress up and act out a community helper's role using the items in the prop box. If props are not available, simply have the children act out the jobs for others to guess. After the others have correctly identified each helper, have the class name two things we trust that helper to do. List these on chart paper under the name of the helper.

Community Helpers Field Trip

Materials:

- paper and pencils
- materials to bind papers into a class booklet (construction paper, stapler, markers, etc.)

Plan a field trip to a police station, fire station, or hospital. Before the trip, ask the children to list things we count on the professionals at that facility to do for the community. Ask several community helpers to talk about how people are depending on them and give examples of situations when they were counted on by others. After returning to the classroom, have the children choose a community helper to write about. Ask each child to pretend he has this job and write about how he helps those who trust him. Allow the children to illustrate their stories. Combine the stories into a booklet titled "Trustworthy Workers." Allow individual children to read the booklet during independent reading time.

"Trust Me" Necklace

Materials:

- Diamond patterns (page 112)
- yarn
- decorative craft materials, such as sequins, glitter, colored paper, crayons, etc.
- glue
- crayons or markers
- scissors

Give each child a copy of the Diamond pattern on page 112. Have him write a short sentence on the diamond describing something he did that was trustworthy. An example could be, "I took the lunch money to the cafeteria for my teacher." (Younger children may need to dictate their sentences for you to write.) Have the child decorate and cut out the pattern. Punch a hole in the top of the diamond and thread a length of yarn through the hole to create a necklace. Encourage the children to proudly wear their "diamond" necklaces.

"Count on Me" Headband

Materials:

- "Count on Me" number pattern (page 112)
- tagboard strips cut to fit around children's heads
- colored paper
- crayons
- glue
- scissors
- stapler

Reproduce the number pattern onto construction paper or other colored paper and give one set to each child. Also give each child a tagboard strip that has been sized to fit around her head. Have the child write, "You can count on me!" Then, have the child glue the numbers to the top of the tagboard strip. Size and staple the strip to fit the child's head. As children wear their hats, have them recite the rhyme, "1, 2, 3, you can count on me!" Then have a child name something that others can count on her to do. Repeat until all children have had a turn.

Trustworthiness Game

Materials:

- paper plates
- white construction paper
- craft sticks
- red and green crayons
- glue
- scissors

Give each student a paper plate and a red and green crayon. Have her color one side of the plate red and the other side of the plate green. Have the student glue a craft stick to the bottom of the plate to make a handle.

Read the following situations to the class. After sharing each story, have students hold up the green sides of their plates if the person in the story acted in trustworthy manner. If the person did not act in a trustworthy manner, have students hold up the red sides and talk about what the person in the story should have done.

Situations:

- Paula's father asked her to walk the dog when she got home from school. Paula told her father that he could count on her to do what he had asked, but when Paula's father got home from work, he found Paula playing with her toys and not walking the dog as she had promised.
- Jason told his classmates that he would meet them at the library to work on their class project. The other students were depending on Jason to bring all of the paper and pencils they needed to finish their report. When the time came for the students to meet, Jason decided he would rather go fishing than go to the library.
- Mrs. Sanders needed a student to collect the money from the school bake sale. Maria volunteered to collect the money. She was very careful to keep the money in a safe place. She made sure to give all of the money to Mrs. Sanders.
- Brad was getting ready to take a math test. He realized he forgot to bring an eraser to class. His friend Lydia said that she had an extra eraser, and that Brad could borrow it for the test. Brad was very careful with the eraser. When the test was over, Brad returned the eraser to Lydia.

Trust Sing-Along

Song:

Sung to the tune of "My Bonnie Lies Over the Ocean"

Trusting your friends is important.
Trust is a good thing, you see.
When I know I can trust you,
Then you know that you can trust me!

Trusting, trusting, trusting each other is good you see.
Trusting, trusting, trust means a lot to me!

Newspaper Stories

Materials:
- chart paper
- handwriting paper
- crayons or markers
- glue
- scissors

Use a marker to write each story starter below on a piece of chart paper. Cut the paper apart so that each story starter is on an individual strip. Divide the class into small groups. Give each group a story starter, then have them read the situation and talk about an ending. Have the group write a rough draft of its story. Then, have each group choose a person to neatly rewrite the story on handwriting paper. Allow the group to illustrate the story. Next, glue the stories on a large piece of chart paper to resemble a newspaper. Encourage the children to think of headlines for the stories. Title the newspaper "Trustworthy Times." Display the newspaper in your classroom.

Story Starters:
- Susan's friends were saying unkind things about her friend Megan. When they asked Susan if she liked Megan, she…
- Sara just got a new bicycle. She told Wendy she could borrow her new bicycle to ride to the park. The bicycle chain broke on the way to the park. Wendy…
- Tony was planning a surprise party for Mark. He told John about the party, but asked him not to tell Mark. When John saw Mark, he…
- Rachel went to buy some candy at the store with her friend Linda. The cashier gave Rachel too much change. Linda told Rachel she should keep the extra money and use it to buy more treats. Rachel…

Trust Walk

Materials:
- an object, such as a chalkboard eraser or book, for each pair of students

Take the class outside to an open area free of obstacles. Have children work in pairs. Ask each pair to stand at one end of the area. Place an object for each pair at the opposite end of the area. Instruct one child in each pair to close his eyes and keep them closed throughout the activity. Have the other child take him gently by the arm, carefully lead him to the object, and guide him in picking up the object and bringing it back to the starting point. Talk with the children about how they had to trust their partners to guide them safely around the area. Talk about the responsibility the partner had in leading the child around. Explain that the partners had to trust each other to get the job done.

Trustworthy Students Bulletin Board

Mrs. Turner's Trustworthy First-Graders!

Amber
1. Wash Dishes.
2. Feed the cat.
3. Brush my teeth.
4. Exercise.

Roger
1. Eat vegetables.
2. Study math.
3. Be honest.
4. Get up on time.

Louise
1. Be on time.
2. Hang up coat.
3. Feed fish.
4. Do homework.

Kathryn
1. Keep promises.
2. Walk the dog.
3. Help others.
4. Clean my room.

Gene
1. Watch my sister.
2. Follow directions.
3. Feed my gerbil.
4. Do my own work.

Give each child a paper plate. Have her draw her face on the plate using crayons or markers, then add hair by gluing colored yarn to the top of the plate. Provide scraps of construction paper, fabric, or wallpaper for the children to use to add details such as collars, hair ribbons, etc. Display the paper plates on a bulletin board. Give each child a piece of writing paper and have her write her name and four things she can be or has been trusted with. Display each child's paper under the appropriate paper plate. Title the display, "(Teacher name)'s Trustworthy (Grade level) Graders!"

Name _____

Trustworthy Choices

Read each sentence. Circle the correct word in the sentence to show you are trustworthy.

1. When I borrow something from you, you know I will (return, keep) it.

2. When I tell you I will meet you somewhere, you know I will (be, not be) there.

3. You can count on me to always (tell the truth, lie).

4. You can count on me to (always, never) cheat.

5. When you tell me a secret, I will tell (everyone, no one).

6. You can count on me to always do what is (wrong, right).

7. If I am on your team, you know I will do my (best, worst).

8. If I found a wallet full of money, I would (keep it, return it).

9. When Mom gives me a chore to do, I (always, never) do it.

10. When I promise to do something, I (will, will not) do it.

Note to Teacher: To make this worksheet appropriate for younger children, read the sentences aloud and have students give oral responses.

Critical Thinking Activity

Read the following story aloud to the class. Have them answer and talk about the questions below.

Juan told Sam that he needed one more player on his football team and said that if Sam did not play, his team would have to forfeit the game. Sam said he would meet Juan after school to play on the team.

Later that day, Alex asked Sam to come to his house to play video games. Sam decided he would rather go to Alex's house than play football, but he had made a promise to Juan.

Sam said to Alex, "I really want to come to your house, but I promised Juan I would meet him after school to play football. Could I come to your house another day?"

Alex agreed, and they played for several hours the next day.

1. What did Sam do that let Juan know he could trust him?

2. How do you think Juan would have felt if Sam had not met him at the football field?

3. Why is it important to keep promises you make to people?

4. What did Sam do to show he wanted to treat Alex fairly?

5. How would you feel about Sam if you were Alex? How would you feel if you were Juan?

6. How do you know Sam is a trustworthy person?

Trustworthiness Patterns

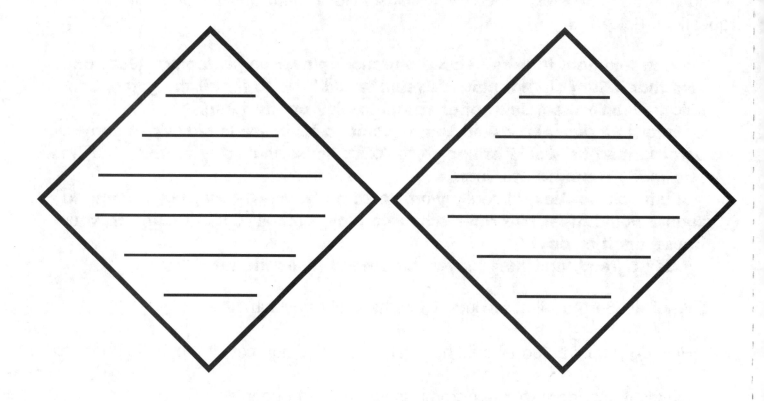

"Count On Me" Headband Pattern